ENDORSEMENTS

"The fear of death can leave us deaf to the truth. In his new book, *No Beginning... No End*, Dr. Terry Gordon reveals a powerful truth: *There is no such thing as death!* The marvelous wisdom and insight he shares are truths my ancestors, the Toltecs, have known for many centuries. This book will forever change your view of life—and death."

~ **don** Miguel Ruiz
Author of *New York Times* bestseller *The Four Agreements* and *The Toltec Art of Life and Death*

"Quantum physics, the most tested and validated of all the sciences, emphasizes that the non-physical energy field, referred to as *consciousness,* shapes our worldly experiences. The greatest fear impacting human consciousness and its influence on health is the belief that death is a termination of existence, a conviction that has a profoundly negative impact on the character of our lives. In contrast, a belief in an eternal, immortal existence (spirituality) has been scientifically shown to significantly enhance an individual's vitality and health.

While most have had a very limited experience of dealing with mortality through the death of a relative or friend, cardiologist Dr. Terry Gordon has personally dealt with death in over a thousand patients. Though Dr. Gordon started his medical career as a non-spiritual conventional scientist, his professional experiences have opened his awareness to the reality that death is simply a transition and not a finality.

In *No Beginning…No End,* Terry's compilation of personal and patient experiences, in conjunction with modern scientific research, documents his evolution into the realm of spiritual immortality. This eminently readable book offers readers an opportunity to move beyond misperceived limitations and fears so that we can write new empowering stories for ourselves, for our children, and for the world. Dr. Terry Gordon's book is a valuable prescription for eliminating fear and enhancing health and happiness!"

~ Bruce H. Lipton, PhD
Cell biologist and author of the bestseller *The Biology of Belief* and *Spontaneous Evolution*

"Dr. Terry Gordon's *No Beginning…No End* is an absolute masterpiece that gives us a new lens for viewing death in its human and cosmic dimensions. Informed by his direct experience as a cardiologist and his evolving spiritual realization, his message shines a radiant light upon the continuity of consciousness. May its revelations bless and bring assurance to your heart."

~ Michael Bernard Beckwith
Author of *Spiritual Liberation* and founder of
AGAPE International Spiritual Center

"As someone who has witnessed the glory of the heavens during three near-death experiences, I can guarantee that you do not need to die in order to understand the message conveyed by cardiologist Dr. Terry Gordon in this most courageous book. Concerned about the lack of spiritual preparation by too many of his patients, Dr. Gordon set out on a profound and altruistic journey to demystify death.

No Beginning…No End offers a treasure trove of wisdom and insight—from the temporal reality of suffering, pain, and grief to more controversial topics such as NDEs and the afterlife.

In this must-read book, Dr. Gordon articulates Truths that will transform your perspective of eternity."

~ Dannion Brinkley
Author of *New York Times* bestseller *Saved by the Light*

"Is survival of consciousness after physical death real? Are we much more than our physical bodies? Does our energy and information, like the light from distant stars, continue and evolve beyond physical death? In this inspiring, heartwarming book, Dr. Gordon shares his professional and personal experiences that support what emerging science is now confirming—there is no death of the mind and personality, only growth and transformation. Written with grace, clarity, vision, and love, this book is a precious gift for all of us. *No Beginning... No End* deserves our careful exploration and celebration."

~ Gary E. Schwartz, PhD

Professor of Psychology, Medicine, Neurology, Psychiatry, and Surgery, at the University of Arizona. Author of *The Afterlife Experiments* and *The Sacred Promise*.

"Dr. Terry Gordon's compelling new book *No Beginning... No End* explores beyond the physical aspect of death where our energy continues, affirming what our Soul already knows: *death is the transformation of consciousness that endures forever.* The wisdom gleaned from these pages will leave the reader with a deeper spiritual understanding of the preciousness of life and how to navigate this world fearlessly. This profound work should be required reading."

~ Caroline Myss

Author of *New York Times* bestseller *Anatomy of the Spirit*

"Devoting his life to keeping people alive, a scientist and renowned cardiologist goes through a spiritual transformation as one of his patients shares with him the truths of the Universe. A shift in consciousness occurs as he discovers new possibilities under the surface of everyday life.

Taking the reader on a soulful journey, Dr. Gordon explores the benefits of living in the moment, near-death experiences, reincarnation, grief, and suffering. As he imparts profound wisdom on these topics, practical and spiritual solutions are revealed in all aspects of life, from birth to death.

Compelling and inspirational, *No Beginning... No End* offers life-changing insights into not only celebrating life, but offers support in overcoming life's most difficult moments."

~ Anita Moorjani
Author of *New York Times* bestseller *Dying to Be Me* and *What If This Is Heaven?*

"I fully resonate with the message Dr. Gordon conveys in his life and death affirming title, *No Beginning... No End.* I have always believed and have experienced the expansion of our consciousness beyond our bodies, beyond death. Dr. Gordon not only discovers, he uncovers the timeless truth that despite the fact that our bodies die, we are truly immortal."

~ Bernie Siegel, MD
New York Times bestselling author of *Love, Medicine and Miracles* and *A Book Of Miracles*

"Dr. Gordon has written an in-depth exploration into the journey of the soul living through its human vehicle. If you've been touched by tragedy, death, terminal illnesses, or loss, you know the abyss it manifests. This book is a guide, a flashlight that helps you to navigate through the darkness. This illuminated path leads a way through to help you learn the lessons of why we are all here. Not just a must read but a must discuss as well."

~ John Edward
Author of *New York Times* bestseller *Crossing Over* and *One Last Time.*

"This groundbreaking book is a must read for those who fear what will happen when death comes knocking at the door. *No Beginning... No End* is a compelling work of irresistible compassion that urges us to embark upon the much-needed spiritual preparation for our demise long before it happens.

Having observed many approach their transition to the other side of life, renowned heart specialist, Dr. Terry Gordon, shares his experiences with us. Once a skeptic himself, he reveals the moment he discovered and accepted the timeless truth: *there is no such thing as death.*

Dr. Gordon provides the reader with a clear road map of the journey, encouraging us to embrace the eternal nature of our soul. If you have ever wondered what will happen when you die, if your fear of the unknown overwhelms you, this book will change your outlook."

~ Joan Borysenko, PhD
New York Times bestselling author of *Minding the Body, Mending the Mind*

"The pain we experience in life is a red badge of courage leading us to one of two destinies—divine knowing or endless suffering. Dr. Terry Gordon is love as he leads us on the path to choosing love over fear with sagacity that could only be gained through his own tumultuous journey. The wisdom he shares in
No Beginning…No End is a gift etched onto your heart and a legacy that is as true as eternity."

~ Scarlett Lewis
Author of *Nurturing Healing Love* and founder of the Jesse Lewis Choose Love Movement

"Dr. Terry Gordon's support for the public placement of Automated External Defibrillators has been of enormous value to our communities. His views on life and death in *No Beginning…No End* are bound to be of interest to many people."

~ Toby Cosgrove, MD
Former President and CEO of The Cleveland Clinic

"Respected cardiologist Dr. Terry Gordon has much experience, both professional and personal, to lend great weight to his observations about life and death. His extraordinary book, *No Beginning…No End,* provides an immense gift to our troubled world, a gift of comfort and understanding about the grand evidence for the reality of the fundamental existence of soul and spirit based on a modern scientific interpretation of the evidence. In so doing, he presents a life-changing opportunity to those open enough to receive his grand wisdom. Highly recommended!"

~ Eben Alexander, MD
Neurosurgeon, author of *New York Times* bestseller
Proof of Heaven and *Living in a Mindful Universe*

"Dr. Terry Gordon provides a poignant view of the human condition and gives the reader thoughtful tools to understand one's ownership and influence over our feelings as we respond to life's healthcare challenges. He is uniquely qualified and fully present in this book, providing personal insight and practical guidance to embrace life's opportunities during our most profound moments of struggle.

Having spent three decades caring for the seriously ill and dying, I feel Dr. Gordon's words provide a guidebook for the heart and the soul. His book reminds us of the beauty that surrounds each of us as well as the strength that lies within us."

~ William E. Finn
President and CEO Hospice of the Western Reserve

"Dr. Terry Gordon is truly a physical and spiritual lifesaver, having spent his years transforming lives as a cardiologist, as a crusader working to keep children safe by placing automated external defibrillators in schools, and now as an author. He has a wonderful ability to humbly share the insights he's gained through his own life journey to light the path for others to follow.

I have been inspired by the powerful stories in *No Beginning… No End*. His heartfelt words connected with me on a profound level and brought to mind memories of my dad. I found myself rereading sections to imagine each situation and fully absorb the message in each chapter. I was especially touched by his wise words on meditation, embracing truth, and eliminating fear. This book is a treasure that needs to be read by all."

~ William Considine
Chief Executive Officer, Retired, Akron Children's Hospital

"*No Beginning... No End* is a beautiful book written by Dr. Terry Gordon. His profound insight on the topic of death will no doubt help alleviate the fear of dying. Dr. Gordon affirms what my brother shared from the 'Afterlife': *there is no such thing as death.* He brilliantly and compassionately guides the reader to this profound understanding. I highly recommend it."

~ Dr. Annie Kagan

Author of the Amazon bestseller, *The Afterlife of Billy Fingers*

"I agree with Dr. Terry Gordon that death doesn't have to be sad. In fact, I've written and spoken extensively across the globe on the topic. As a clown, I've been able to help bring a smile to the faces of 10,000 people on their deathbeds. I'm actually quite fun to die with!

I so appreciate Dr. Gordon's book, *No Beginning... No End* as a grand midwife and companion to those transitioning. My advice is relax, and most of all, be sure to delight in living. Welcome to eternity."

~ Patch Adams, MD

Author of *Gesundheit!: Bringing Good Health to You, the Medical System, and Society through Physician Service, Complementary Therapies, Humor, and Joy*

NO BEGINNING ... NO END

A Cardiologist Discovers There Is No Such Thing as Death

DR. TERRY GORDON

Waterside Productions

Printed in the United States of America

First Printing, 2021

ISBN-13: 978-1-954968-12-7 print edition
ISBN-13: 978-1-954968-13-4 ebook edition

Waterside Productions
2055 Oxford Ave
Cardiff, CA 92007
www.waterside.com

DEDICATION

To all of the gentle souls who have forged paths to eternity, thank you for helping prepare the rest of us for the journey.

TABLE OF CONTENTS

ACKNOWLEDGMENTS

I am forever grateful to Sarah Friebert, MD, for her enormous contribution in helping to bring my manuscript to life. I am even more admiring of her life's work as Director of Palliative Care at Akron Children's Hospital, appreciating the many lives she has so tenderly touched.

To my father—your valiant will to live, the courage and fortitude you displayed as the time of your transition approached provided a plethora of invaluable lessons for those of us who were blessed to be in your circle. From your tutorial, *No Beginning... No End* has come to fruition. It will no doubt help many others as they face the sum of their greatest fears.

From them and from me, Dad... Thank you.

To Mom—Your recent transition to the next phase of life will serve as a rich template for the rest of us to follow. I pray your journey back to the place from where you have come will be an enlightening passage, one filled with sweet silence as the Universe welcomes you back and shares with you all of its secrets. Shalom dear Bebbe.

FOREWORD

By Larry Dossey, MD

New York Times bestselling author of *One Mind: How Our Individual Mind Is Part of a Greater Consciousness and Why It Matters*

The only secret people keep is immortality.
~ Emily Dickinson

The fear of death has probably caused more suffering in human history than all the physical diseases combined. In our attempts to cope with this grim inevitability, we humans have traditionally looked to religious and spiritual sources for solace against the impending destruction of everything that is "I." In recent decades, powerful reinforcements to faith have appeared. They are the subject of this important book.

A personal note: While reading Dr. Terry Gordon's manuscript, I was riveted by the similarity of his and my personal journeys. While Dr. Gordon practiced invasive cardiology after being trained at the world-famous Cleveland Clinic and I practiced internal medicine at a major urban hospital, many of the following pages describe nearly identical experiences we've shared with sick and dying patients, resuscitations, and medical emergencies. Dr. Gordon looked beyond these experiences to explore larger lessons dealing with spirituality, transcendent meaning, and the infinite continuity of consciousness pre-birth and post-death. These have long been my concerns as well. So I immediately recognized in Dr. Gordon not just a professional colleague but a spiritual brother as well.

For too long, healthcare professionals have considered spiritual and religious issues as matters to be addressed only by a minister, priest, or rabbi, but not by a physician, surgeon, or nurse. As a result, immortality is not a topic discussed in the medical literature. This view is changing rapidly, however, because of an avalanche of information pointing toward the infinite, nonlocal, unitary, and eternal nature of consciousness. [1, 2, 3, 4]

Carl G. Jung, the great Swiss psychiatrist, was a pioneer in addressing immortality. He observed, "As a doctor, I make every effort to strengthen the belief in immortality..." [5] However, some decry this development. They warn that physicians, nurses, and other healthcare professionals should not get involved with spirituality because they are not trained to do so.[6] Similar warnings were issued a few years ago about physician involvement in sexuality. The sexual lives of our patients were too sensitive and personal for us to enter, it was said, and we had no skills in this area. But the epidemic of AIDS and sexually transmitted diseases swept away these objections overnight. No one is suggesting that healthcare professionals usurp the role of hospital chaplains, ministers, priests, and rabbis. However, there is no reason we can't work collaboratively with our clerical colleagues. We don't have to be experts in spiritual care to deliver a bit of it. Just as we teach laypersons a basic level of competence in CPR without expecting them to be cardiologists or heart surgeons, healthcare professionals can acquire basic levels of competence in "spiritual medicine" without becoming pros.[7]

I have long believed that a factor obstructing the recognition of the importance of spirituality in health is a dour, depressive, and humorless attitude toward this subject in general. This may be unavoidable in view of the fear that *nothing* survives death. But if the scientific and clinical evidence for survival were taken seriously, we should be joyful. So over the years, I've collected some light-hearted observations pointing to the need for a more cheerful attitude. Here is a sample of them.

Almost everyone is burningly curious about what happens when we die. Take 28-year-old Ben Rock, one of the student moviemakers of the 1999 American transcendental horror film *The Blair Witch Project*. After the low-budget movie proved wildly popular and shocked Hollywood, interviewers sought out the young filmmakers to find out what made them tick. One interviewer asked them, "If there was one Great Question you'd like answered, what would that be?" Rock replied, "I would like to know what actually happens after we die. Do we float away from our bodies attached to an endless silver thread, do we go to heaven or Valhalla, or does our brain simply short out and our consciousness end?" Rock's concern was not shared by Daniel Myrick, one of his colleagues on the film project. For him, the Great Question was, "Which one's the salad fork? It's about time I knew the answer."[8]

Television is particularly revealing of what our culture thinks about the afterlife. While channel surfing one day, I stumbled onto a discussion of immortality on a talk show. "Do they wear clothes over there?" the hostess asked her invited expert. I was immediately riveted. The guest had written a monster bestseller about her near-death experience, which involved what she believed was a visit to heaven. She replied thoughtfully that, although she couldn't speak for everyone, *she* certainly wasn't naked during her journey. Then someone from the audience asked, without a hint of humor, whether the clothes they wore in heaven were togas or something a bit more contemporary. In this amazing conversation, the *fact* of survival was completely taken for granted; how people *looked* was the hot topic. You've got to admire that sort of attention to detail.

On balance, I'm not all that interested in the nitpicking details of the hereafter. My main concern is whether or not consciousness survives, period. It's the big picture that counts. I assume that a universal intelligence that would provide for the continuation of consciousness can also handle the dress code, the menu, and the activity schedule.

In fact, I find the traditional images of heaven a turnoff, and I'm not alone. As a result of my writings about spiritual issues in medicine, people often share with me their most intimate thoughts of the afterlife, and many of them are troubled. One man told me he dreads the thought of being eternally exposed to harp music, which he loathes. One woman who is afraid of heights is phobic about floating around on porous clouds. Some of the most interesting letters I receive are from prisoners. One inmate in a federal prison wrote of his concern about those *keys* to the Pearly Gates. This image suggests to him a state of perpetual lockdown, and this bothers him tremendously. One of the most uptight individuals I know is concerned whether he can adjust to the *boredom* of heaven, should he be fortunate enough to wind up there. A mom said that her child, who suffers from an allergy to feathers, asked whether this poses a problem if she goes to heaven and finds herself surrounded by angels with wings. Several pet lovers say their priest has told them animals don't have souls and therefore are not candidates for heaven. Because many pet owners consider their animals more deserving than most humans, this suggests to them that the Divine is unjust. This reminds me of a comment by Will Rogers, the American humorist: "If there are no dogs in heaven, then when I die I want to go where they went."

Some of the people who are turned off by the traditional images of heaven appear to be genuine introverts. They are concerned that heaven sounds a lot like a permanent social event designed by and for extraverts, with all that strolling, chatting, and singing—thus Tennyson's line, "Heard the heavens fill with shouting…"[9] "For people who like this sort of thing," Abe Lincoln once quipped in another context, "this is the sort of thing they will like." But what if one *doesn't* like this sort of thing? They worry that no one ever emphasizes *privacy* in heaven. Is heaven the end of solitude? Can you still go to your room up there? I am sympathetic with their concern. In all the religious and spiritual literature dealing with the afterlife I've read, I can't recall a single instance in which privacy issues are discussed. It's as if you've got to take the Myers-Briggs personality test and be branded an extravert before being admitted.

Don't think these concerns are limited to the common folk. Many intellectuals are so concerned about the details of the afterlife that they think annihilation might be better than survival. An example is the influential Cambridge philosopher C. D. Broad. He was thoroughly informed about research in the field of parapsychology and the implications of these findings for an afterlife. He figured the odds were at least fifty-fifty for some form of survival following death, yet he did not find this a happy thought. He considered this world a nasty place and fretted that the next one might be even worse. Consequently, he wryly observed that if he died and found himself still conscious, he would be "slightly more annoyed than surprised."[10] Karl Barth, the Swiss theologian, seemed concerned that the admission policy of heaven might be too liberal. He asserted that God did not create heaven for geese.[11] One wonders how he knew.

The disdain of many intellectuals toward the afterlife implies that there is something wrong with the rest of us: we are too scared and weak-willed to face our impending doom. It may be the other way 'round: there may be something wrong with *them*. I have long suspected that people who are repelled by the idea of immortality may be suffering from subclinical agoraphobia. Just as agoraphobics are horrified of open spaces, the immortality haters seem terrified of the *infinitude* that is suggested by immortality—all that space and time. As permanent treatment for their disorder, they prefer confinement in a cozy grave where they stay put forever, without being disturbed by even a glimmer of consciousness.

Now to more serious concerns. Some objectors to immortality are downright hostile to the possibility of survival. They say the desire for immortality implies a weakness of character or a philosophical sellout. This attitude is apparent in philosopher Bertrand Russell's famous comment: "I believe that when I die I shall rot, and nothing of my ego will survive. But I should scorn to shiver with terror at the thought of annihilation. Happiness is nonetheless true happiness because it must come to an end, nor do thought and love lose their value because they are not everlasting."[12]

Some philosophers find the idea of life after death morally repellent because the concept is so often connected with rewards and punishments. Even spiritual teachers have criticized people's motives for desiring heaven. An example is the eighth-century Sufi poet Rabia Basri who once walked the Arabian Desert with fire in one hand and water in the other. She said she would quench the fires of hell and set fire to heaven so that humans would love God neither from fear of hell nor from hope of paradise but only from pure love.[13]

Many are repulsed by the idea that people who behave poorly through no fault of their own or because of extenuating circumstances might be barred from heaven. Others find it irrational that some type of hellish punishment might go on forever. There comes a point, they say, where even the most heinous crime is paid off, the scales of justice are balanced, and punishment should cease. Another common objection to life after death is that this belief is essentially an opiate; if people have their attention fixed on the hereafter, this may undermine their passion to achieve justice for everyone in this life. Similarly, a fixation on the future might make people complacent about the fate of Earth in the face of nuclear, environmental, and other threats. Some say that belief in eternal life leads to apocalyptic thinking and that those who believe in immortality might try to bring down the curtain on this existence in order to usher in the next one.

But even if we combine all the objections to the afterlife, they are swamped by the overwhelming conviction of humans worldwide, in all eras, that, following death, there's something more. Are these beliefs substantial, or are they wishful thinking?

In a nutshell, immortality implies that consciousness is more than the physical brain and body. For many paid-up scientists and philosophers, this is heresy. For if consciousness is more than the brain, then many cherished concepts in modern science are simply wrong. As philosopher Colin McGinn describes the view of the contemporary materialistic scientist:

> What we call "the mind" is in fact made up of a great number
> of sub-capacities, and each of these depends upon the func-
> tioning of the brain. [The facts of neurology] compellingly

demonstrate ... that everything about the mind, from the sensory-motor periphery to the inner sense of self, is minutely controlled by the brain. If your brain lacks certain chemicals or gets locally damaged, your mind is apt to fall apart at the seams ... If parts of the mind depend for their existence upon parts of the brain, then the whole of the mind must so depend too. Hence the soul dies with the brain, which is to say it is mortal.[14]

Fortunately, as Dr. Gordon shows, the denunciation by scientists of an infinite, eternal, nonlocal form of consciousness that points toward immortality is softening. One reason is the recognition of our appalling ignorance about what consciousness *is*. A growing number of scientific insiders openly admit that, where consciousness is concerned, we simply don't know what we are talking about. For instance, John Searle, a distinguished philosopher in the field of consciousness studies, has acknowledged that, "At our present state of the investigation of consciousness, we *don't know* how it works and we need to try all kinds of different ideas."[15] Philosopher Jerry A. Fodor similarly observes, "Nobody has the slightest idea how anything material could be conscious. Nobody even knows what it would be like to have the slightest idea about how anything material could be conscious. So much for the philosophy of consciousness."[16] Sir John Maddox, a former editor of the prestigious journal *Nature,* soberly stated, "The catalogue of our ignorance must include the understanding of the human brain ... What consciousness consists of ... is ... a puzzle. Despite the marvelous success of neuroscience in the past century, we seem as far away from understanding as we were a century ago. The most important discoveries of the next 50 years are likely to be ones of which we cannot now even conceive."[17] And cognitive psychologist Donald Hoffman of the University of California-Irvine observes, "The scientific study of consciousness is in the embarrassing position of having no scientific theory of consciousness."[18]

By now, many people realize that the modern views of space and time are fundamentally different from the views held by most of our predecessors. As physicist Paul Davies states, "No physical experiment has ever been performed to detect the passage of time. As soon as the objective world of reality is considered, the passage of time disappears like a ghost into the night. [19] Yet, for most westerners, time is still experienced as a flowing entity—the "river of time"—that passes in an irreversible, one-way direction. We carve this river up into segments we call past, present, and future. Consequently, we say we only live once; death is final because we cannot go backward in time and recapture life. As composer Hector Berlioz put it, "Time is a great teacher, but unfortunately it kills all its pupils." But immortality presumes a different view of time. Immortal things are outside of time; they have no beginning and no end and are not "running down."

The view of time that is emerging from quantum-relativistic science is more cordial to the idea of a nonlocal, timeless view of consciousness than the older views, and therefore are more favorable for immortality. As physicist David Bohm stated, "Ultimately all the moments are really one ... therefore now is eternity ... Everything, including me, is dying every moment into eternity and being born again ... "[20]

Finally, what about the objection that belief in the afterlife will cause people to become unbalanced, irresponsible, dreamy mystics; that they may forget to eat or change the baby's diapers? Philosopher David Griffin suggests a different view. He offers several practical benefits of a belief in an afterlife:

- Such a belief can help overcome the fear of death and extermination.
- If people are convinced they are ultimately not subject to any earthly power, this can increase their courage to fight for freedom, ecologically sustainable policies, and social justice.
- If people believe that this life is not the final word and that justice will prevail in the next life, this can help them withstand the unfairness they encounter in the here and now.

- The idea of life as an ongoing journey, which continues even after death, can lead to a greater sense of connection with the universe as it unfolds into the future.
- The belief in life after death can help counter the extreme degree of materialism that has invaded every niche of modern civilization.

The belief that we are on a spiritual journey and that we have time to reach our destination can motivate us to think creatively about what we can do now—socially, internationally, and individually—to move closer to what we should be in the here-and-now.[21]

Griffin believes that a belief in the next life is one of our best hopes of improving this one—indeed, of having a future on Earth. As he puts it:

I believe the human race now faces the greatest challenge in its history. If it continues on its present course, widespread misery and death of unprecedented proportions is a certainty within the next century or two. Annihilation of human life, and of millions of other species as well, is probable. This is so because of polluting technologies, economic growth-mania, out-of-control population growth, global apartheid between rich and poor nations, rapid depletion of nonrenewable resources, and proliferation of nuclear weapons combined with a state of international anarchy that makes war inevitable and sufficient measures to halt global ecological destruction impossible.

...What seems clear...is that...a transition in world *order*, if it is to occur, will have to be accompanied by a widespread shift in world*view*, one that would lead to a new sense of adventure, one replacing the modern adventure of unending economic growth based on the technological subjugation of nature and the military and/or economic subjugation of weaker peoples. Only, I am convinced, if we come to see human life as primarily a spiritual adventure, an adventurous journey that continues beyond this life, will we have a chance of becoming sufficiently free from destructive motivations to effect a transition to a sustainable global order.[22]

The majority of the medical schools in the United States have developed courses dealing with spiritual issues in health. This shows dramatically that the taboo on spirituality in medicine has been broken. When the history of this transition is written, Dr. Terry Gordon will occupy an honored place.

So as you peruse this book, I hope you will bear in mind the larger picture. You are now participating in a turning point in human knowing—the moment in history in which the fear of the extermination of consciousness with death began to curl back on itself toward an affirmation of the infinite extent and duration of consciousness; a turning point based not just in faith but also in objective findings about the fundamental nature of consciousness; a movement toward hope, joy, and a celebration of life; a resolve to hand forward this understanding to those who follow us; and a determination to preserve the precious cradle of our existence, this great Earth, because we now sense the sacred, shimmering glow permeating a Universe that provides immortality and infinitude for its inhabitants.

Know this, dear reader: Immortality does not kick in at the moment of physical death. Immortality involves *infinite* duration in time: no beginning, no end, just as Dr. Gordon maintains.

That means you and I are *already* immortal. *Now.*

Think about that.

~ Larry Dossey, MD
New York Times bestselling author of *One Mind: How Our Individual Mind Is Part of a Greater Consciousness and Why It Matters*

PREFACE

O ne of the most defining moments in my life occurred early in my career as a cardiologist. I was in the operating room during an open-heart procedure. Cradling the patient's beating heart in my hands, I could feel the pulsation of each contraction. I experienced utter amazement at how that organ knew *when* to beat. I marveled at the energy it must take to drive the heart day after day, year after year, and decade after decade.

The heart somehow possessed an understanding of nature and knowledge of the Universe, conveying with each beat its connection with the Source of all creation. I became mesmerized by its rhythm: thump-thummmp ... thump-thummmp ... thump-thummmp.

Throughout my medical career, which spanned over a quarter century, I was blessed to practice in an exciting era of many innovations. My training as an invasive cardiologist at the Cleveland Clinic coincided with a period of discovery that quite literally changed the landscape of medicine. During my tenure, advances included such life-enhancing procedures as angioplasty and coronary stenting, the development of the artificial heart, successful heart transplantation, and the invention of the implantable defibrillator, a device that delivers a life-saving shock to the heart. Despite being a part of these exciting times, I have many regrets—over a thousand of them.

I have witnessed many people taking their last breath. Usually, I was one of the physicians frantically trying to keep alive the person who had suffered a cardiac arrest. When a "Code Blue" was announced over the hospital PA system, caregivers would rush to the patient's bedside, the goal being resuscitation. The essentially dead patient would be jabbed with needles. Medication would be pushed intravenously, on occasion injected directly into the heart. A tube would be inserted into the airway while the patient's chest would be forcibly compressed and jolted with multiple electric shocks. A nurse would chart the vital signs carefully documenting what could well be the patient's last moments of life.

Some would be revived; others would not. For the latter, when all efforts had been exhausted, the patient would be pronounced dead, and the process would come to an end with everyone returning to the tasks they were involved with prior to the emergency.

Training and objective reaction are critically important to physicians who need to make split-second life and death decisions without emotional interference. Too often encumbered by mammoth workloads and time constraints, or perhaps as a defense mechanism, physicians do not have the time, nor perhaps do we even wish to contemplate what is *really* happening at the precise moment we commonly refer to as death. The sorrow I feel and my greatest regret lie in the fact that for most of my career, I was oblivious to the spiritual aspect of the so-called "dying" patient's transition to the next phase of life. But, as the saying goes: better late than never.

An enlightening realization occurred to me close to the end of my cardiology career. I had read tens of thousands of EKGs or electrocardiograms. But during the countless hours I spent doing so, I never once contemplated what I am about to share with you.

It was late one evening after a very long day. My mind was numb as I began the task of tackling the large pile of over 400 EKGs that had accrued over the course of the day. As I began the process of interpreting one after another, I soon settled into a zone, a meditative state that allowed the reading of these electrocardiograms to flow with ease.

When an EKG is performed, electrodes are placed on the surface of the chest, arms, and ankle. These leads become receivers of the electromagnetic energy generated by the heart. Because no two hearts are alike, each individual EKG inscribes its own unique signature.

I began contemplating what it takes to create an electrocardiogram. Years before in medical school, I had been taught the physiology of what drives each heart beat. The body's mineral consistency and 80 percent water content provide an excellent milieu for conduction of electrical impulses.

Electrical excitation causes the heart muscle to contract, propelling enriched, life-sustaining blood throughout the body. I thought about how, on a beat-by-beat basis, this life force enlightens each and every cell in the body to the nature of its heart, constantly circulating and recirculating this vital information day in and day out for as long as that particular physical form survives in the material realm.

My meditative state deepened, as I *became* that electrical impulse spreading through the body, exciting everything in its path. I pondered the place of its creation and how it knew what it needed in order to fulfill its destiny. And, just as intriguing, I contemplated where each electrical impulse was headed.

For the first time in my career, I wondered what happens to that electromotive force once an impulse is transmitted to the electrodes at the end of our arms and legs and the EKG is written. Does the energy of the impulse suddenly hit an obstruction halting its further transmission?

The answer is no. On its outward-bound path, rippling out into the Universe, the impulse continues. Similar to every other electromagnetic impulse, our heart's voice travels at the speed of light, 186,000 miles per second. After only one minute, each heartbeat's signal has the potential to travel more than 11,000,000 miles from its beacon point!

Every impulse emanating from each beating heart, whether human or belonging to a blue whale or a fairy fly becomes as much a part of the cosmos as the most powerful photons emitted from the largest stars. Some of those stars died millions of years ago, yet their essence continues as the twinkling light we observe as their energy traverses through the vast Universe heading in our direction. Granted, the impulse of the heart is not nearly as strong as that of a star, but the heart's voice, soft as it may be, travels in the very same vacuum of space … forever! Indeed, the heart's imprint is like that of the stars; it never ceases to be.

It was at this moment when I first acknowledged the epiphany: *There is no such thing as death.*

I was thrilled when I discovered that Gary Schwartz, PhD, in *The Afterlife Experiments* offered groundbreaking scientific evidence that supported my evolving understanding of life after death.

For many, the greatest fear we experience is of our own demise. The very notion of death can be paralyzing. We find ourselves discouraged by the prospect of losing independence and having to rely on others for our most basic needs. We dread the indignity of the physical and psychological ravages disease might impart on us, and we fear losing what we have relied on the most throughout our lives to define who we are—our healthy and vibrant bodies.

We find ourselves mourning what we perceive to be the finality of a death that appears to separate us forever from those people and places we love the most.

But what if there is no such thing as death? What if life and its energetic essence do indeed survive what we have been taught to accept as the end of the road? In the pages that follow, the word *death* is not intended to describe a discrete or finite occurrence in linear time. Instead, I invite you to consider *death* as simply a transfer of energy, a natural corollary of life, a necessary passageway to eternity.

Some of the names mentioned in this book have been changed in order to protect the privacy of my patients and their families. For the same reason, I have also taken literary license to change small parts of some of their stories. Similarities to other individuals who are currently alive or have previously transitioned are unintentional.

As a retired cardiologist, I do not dispense medical advice or prescribe the use of any technique as a form of treatment for physical, emotional, or medical problems. The intent of

No Beginning...No End is to offer information of a general nature to help in your quest for emotional and spiritual well-being. Should you use any of the information in this book for yourself, the author and the publisher assume no responsibility for your actions.

I am neither a hospice physician nor a grief counselor. I am simply an observer who has been blessed to be at the bedside of many as they continued their journey to the next phase of life.

My humble prayer is that as we journey together through the pages to follow, *there is no such thing as death* will become as much an awakening for you as it has been for this scientist. As you traverse the path before you, I trust my words will bring many blessings to you.

Namaste,
Dr. Terry Gordon

PART I:

THE BIRTH OF BIRTH

CHAPTER 1

THE SHIFT

As children, we are introduced in subtle fashion to the harsh reality of life and death. Looking back at the movies and fairy tales I was exposed to in my youth, I recall the horror I felt as a youngster sitting in a movie theater watching Walt Disney's movie, *Bambi*. During his first winter of life, Bambi and his mother are out foraging for food when a hunter approaches. The mother alerts her infant of the danger as they both bolt in the direction away from the deer hunter. Shots are fired as Bambi makes it to the safety of the underbrush, turning around and exclaiming, "We made it, Mother! We made it!" Then, realizing that his mother is not with him, he hesitantly calls out, "Mother? Mother, where are you?"

Alone in the dark snowy forest, he wanders aimlessly in search of his protector, too young to be able to comprehend that his mother has been shot and killed by a hunter. In one last desperate attempt to find her, Bambi cries out, "Mother, please come back."

From the darkness of night, a buck appears and says, "Bambi, your mother cannot be with you anymore."

I remember feeling the knot in my throat when Bambi's innocent eyes well up with tears as he looks back into the emptiness of the forest with the buck softly encouraging him: "Come, my son."

That was my first experience with death. The innocence of youth would never be the same for me as I learned about the apparent finality of life from the silver screen. It would become the lesson that would prepare me ultimately to face literally thousands of people as they died. Fear of this unknown would become fodder for growth and ultimately offer me a more complete understanding of life and the transition we must all face.

My interest in cardiology was piqued as a youngster while watching a documentary on television about a boy who was born with a large hole in his heart. Although he and I were only five years apart in age, the difference between us was dramatic. I was very active physically. Not only could he not run, he could barely walk six feet without turning blue. In order to catch his breath, he would have to squat and breathe through pursed lips for several minutes before he could stand up and continue for another few steps. Then he would have to stop once again and repeat the maneuver. This was the first time I recall not only becoming aware of my many blessings but also of being grateful for them as well.

The documentary projected on our black-and-white TV revealed his doctors subjecting their young patient to a myriad of tests in order to formulate a working diagnosis of his tenuous medical condition. The methodical process of working up a cardiac malady captivated me. As complicated as it seemed, there was a beautiful simplicity to the way the heart worked.

Watching the open-heart surgery on this young boy, I felt an exhilaration I had never before experienced. Weeks after his surgery, he was able to walk and play like any other child his age. I marveled at how a single surgical procedure could so dramatically improve the quality of life.

The scientist seed in me had been sown. The foundation of what I was to become continued to blossom as every book report, every school project assigned, and even the plastic models I built were centered on this beautiful piece of machinery, the human heart. My intention, although I didn't know how to describe it so early in life, was to become a heart doctor.

Perhaps not so coincidentally, that same summer, two significant people in my life died. I was away at summer camp when I received the message that my grandfather had died. PawPaw had been living with us after sustaining a stroke several years before while living in rural Crofton, Kentucky.

I returned home that very day. My mother picked me up at the airport and drove us to the funeral home to pick up my father.

Not having been around death before, I really didn't know what to expect. When we arrived at the funeral home, Dad was sitting on the ground sobbing. This disturbed me, as I had never before seen Dad cry. He came from a time when men generally didn't show emotions. Although I couldn't digest at the time what he was enduring, it would be only 12 years later when my own father succumbed to metastatic prostate cancer that I felt the pain, the fear, and the loneliness he must have been experiencing the day his father died. Regardless of how old we are when our parents die, we become orphans.

Several months later, I called my best friend, Johnny Perlstein, who had been undergoing treatment for leukemia. He had missed the first few weeks of school, so I called him that Sunday night to see how he was doing. In the course of our conversation, I shared with him how excited I was to learn that he'd be returning to school the following morning. He told me he was already in bed and that his mother had set out his school stuff for him in anticipation of his return.

When he didn't show up at school the next morning, I assumed he just wasn't feeling up to it. But Johnny would never return to school. After our conversation the night before, Johnny had gone to sleep. Sometime during the night, my best friend succumbed to his disease. Being the last of his friends to talk with him weighed heavily on my heart for many years. Could I have said more? Did Johnny feel my love for him? Did he appreciate the impact his life and death would have on me?

It was extremely difficult for me to grasp his death, but on a deeply personal level that morning, I learned at the age of ten how tenuous and fragile life could be. I questioned how someone could be there one moment and, in a flash, be gone forever.

One thing was for sure—at this young age, I wanted then more than ever to become a physician. My desire was to facilitate the healing of others, to assuage their suffering, and, if possible, to help keep people from dying. Although my aspirations seemed clear, my end game was flawed.

Training to become a physician is laborious and time-consuming, but it was a process of growth and learning that I found absolutely invigorating! Seventeen years after graduating high school, I had completed four years of college at Emory University, two years of post-baccalaureate studies, four years of medical school, a year of internship, three years of residency, and three years of fellowship in invasive cardiology at the Cleveland Clinic. I emerged a well-trained scientist. My studies included anatomy, physiology, biology, neurology, pathology, and many other science-based courses, all of which helped mold me as a physician. These courses offered the facts that would enable me to effectively practice evidence-based medicine.

While science taught me to accept as fact that which my five senses experienced, it would take years for me to discover the fallacy of that approach.

I came to appreciate that invariably facts change. New revelations and technological advances open doors to discoveries that undermine previously held positions based on what we thought we knew. These old "truths" change when the facts supporting them change. As an example, prior to the invention of the microscope, scientists couldn't see bacteria or viruses. That, of course, didn't preclude the existence of such pathogens.

An interesting shift occurred in this scientist about 20 years ago. As an invasive cardiologist, my pace was a grueling one. Beginning at 6:45 a.m., I would perform the first of perhaps five or six heart catheterizations, do a couple of angioplasties and stents, and maybe implant a pacemaker. In between procedures, I would see the 30-40 patients hospitalized under my care, finishing in time to get to my office by 1:30 p.m. to see another 15-20 patients in the afternoon.

One morning I was in the middle of a typical day of hospital rounds. I had literally run from one patient's room to another with a trail of medical students and residents trying to keep up with me. Quickly perusing the chart of a new patient I was about to see, I paused, took in a deep breath, and with a façade of calmness, entered his room.

Art Blair was a friendly guy who had been admitted to the hospital the previous evening with a heart rhythm disturbance called atrial fibrillation. As I entered his room, the first thing out of his mouth was, "Whoa, Dr. Gordon, you're killing yourself!"

I was taken aback, to say the least. My response was, "I beg your pardon?"

He said it again: "You're killing yourself, Doc. I can see your aura. You are surrounded by marvelous energy, but it's terribly fractured. Man, you'd better do something about this," he said, slowly shaking his head, "or something very bad is going to happen to you."

I really didn't have time for this. In a nice way I shared with him, "You know Mr. Blair, *I'm* the doctor. *I'm* here to help *you*, not the other way around!"

Art was a persistent sort. Not letting go, he offered, wagging his finger at me, "Well okay, but you'd better slow down."

Once I completed his examination and shared with him my plan of treatment, I turned to leave his room, my thoughts already focused on the next patient I was to see. On my way out, Mr. Blair beckoned to me: "You know, Doc, when the student is ready, the teacher will appear."

I didn't respond to his comment as I left his room, but I remember thinking, *what the hell is this old geezer talking about?*

Art was discharged several days later, only to return again in a couple of months with the same complaints of fluttering in his chest. His atrial fibrillation had returned.

It was during that hospitalization he once again pressed me to make a change in my modus operandi, offering several helpful suggestions. He recommended that I learn how to meditate, telling me, "You realize, Doc, meditation would benefit you immensely. It would help you to reconnect with your higher self, ya know, the one that somewhere along the way you've forgotten." He also suggested that I read a couple of books, *Real Magic* and *Inspiration* by Dr. Wayne Dyer.

Three months later, Art presented to the hospital, this time experiencing excruciating chest discomfort. My suspicion was that he had significant blockages in the arteries supplying his heart. So the next morning, I took him to the lab to perform a cardiac catheterization. As I made the preparations to begin his procedure, an emergency arose in the coronary care unit; another patient was having a major heart attack. We had to abort Art's catheterization, triaging in order to attend to this more pressing emergency.

About halfway through that two-hour angioplasty and stenting procedure, I stepped out into the hallway just to make sure Art was doing okay. He was seemingly asleep on the gurney in the hallway and in no apparent distress.

When I was finally able to get Art back into the lab to begin his procedure, I apologized for the delay. He responded with a radiant smile and with an almost musical tone to his voice, "No problem, Doc. I had two hours of GREAT meditation!" Then he added, "Do you want to know what I saw in my meditative state?"

Not waiting for my response, he continued, "I saw that you are going to find two blockages in my heart."

I smiled at him as I responded: "Well, Mr. Hotshot Meditator Man, let's see how good you are!" I had performed thousands of these procedures, never knowing for sure what I'd find until I got in and actually visualized the arteries. I laughed to myself because this weird dude who had never so much as seen a heart catheterization was telling me—someone who had performed over 8,000 procedures—what I was going to find! It was amusing, to say the least.

As I completed his procedure, Art must have seen a smile cross my face because he asked, "What's so funny, Doc?"

"Well, Art," I paused, "perhaps we should have delayed your catheterization for three hours rather than just two so that you would have had more time to meditate on what you really have." I then added rather cavalierly, "There's just one blockage."

Art wouldn't let go. "Are you sure, Doc?" he asked. "I know I saw two blockages in my meditation."

I reviewed the films with him frame by frame, which showed that in each view, there was only one blockage. It was a critical blockage, but I assured him there was only one occlusion.

What happened next brought gooseflesh crawling over my skin as Art looked at me with such conviction, his crystal hazel eyes pierced mine as he slowly said, emphasizing each word, "Terry, you're missing something."

I remember the nurse who was assisting me poking me in the ribs with her elbow, a perplexed look of uncertainty in her eyes. I reviewed his films with him one more time, but he remained insistent that I had missed one of his blockages.

To get him off my back, I took one additional view of his arteries at an angle I rarely take.

Guess what I found? The second blockage!

How did he know? He had no training in anatomy. He hadn't been educated in the sciences I had relied on for all these years. But somehow Art *knew*.

I fixed his two clogged arteries, stenting them successfully, but I must share with you, I don't recall performing the procedure. My mind was elsewhere. The question kept scrolling through my mind. *How did he know there were two blockages? Was I missing something?*

When I finished Art's procedure, I bolted to my office. I couldn't wait to finish seeing patients in the office that afternoon. Intrigue was drawing me back to Art like a powerful magnet. I sensed I was about to be introduced to something very profound.

When I finally completed my 14-hour day, I went straight to Art's room. Entering, I threw my hands in the air and admitted, "Alright, man, you've got my attention. What's this all about?"

Art and I spent the evening together in his hospital room as he shared with me some of the truths he had come to know while traversing his spiritual path.

The dawn of a new way of thinking had been gently introduced to me as Art made me open my eyes to new possibilities that lay way beyond my previous comfort zone. He showed me that I was indeed missing something, actually a lot of somethings! Up to this point, I had been recalcitrant, so frozen in my way of processing that I couldn't see beyond what was right in front of my eyes. But Art encouraged me to open my eyes in order to acknowledge the path charted for me by the Universe.

I could feel a change of heart unfolding. The time had come for a shift in my consciousness. Years of training and experience had paved the way for this precise moment. I made the conscious decision to take a step most scientists refuse to consider. I chose to *be open to everything and attached to nothing.* A new facet of my life's journey had presented itself, one that would lead me to the discovery of unimaginable Truths.

The student was ready, and with Divine orchestration, a teacher had appeared.

WHISPERS OF THE HEART:

1. Be open to everything and attached to nothing. Imagine the fresh perspective achievable as you become unencumbered by the very attachments that have previously obscured your enlightenment. Instead, try to purposefully look at your circumstance in a way totally different from the way you have done so before. See if you notice a change in what you perceive.

2. When the student is ready, the teacher will appear. Enlightenment cannot be rushed. It will begin to unfold only when your heart and soul reach the place of being open to such change.

3. In anticipation of a shift in consciousness, be receptive to the energetic messages coming your way from the Universe.

CHAPTER 2

BECOMING

I have witnessed the first breath taken by a newborn baby. I have also observed the last breath taken by many older individuals as they die. That which exists between these two bookends of our lives, the first and last breath, has challenged me to seek a greater understanding of the perplexing questions involving why we are here, from where have we come, as well as why we must depart and where we go when we leave.

As a medical student and early in my training as a physician, I spent several months on the obstetrics and gynecology services. It was during those rotations that I was privileged to observe and participate in the births of many babies, the vast majority of them entering this world healthy. My training occurred during a time when diagnostic ultrasound of pregnant women and genetic testing of fetuses were both in their infancy.

One morning, a lady presented full-term to the labor and delivery unit. This was her first pregnancy, and she had experienced no complications. The fetus had steadily grown, apparently in normal fashion; all seemingly was in order for a healthy baby to be born to thrilled parents-to-be.

The delivery room usually has an anticipatory excitement in the air, shared by all present whose purpose it is to facilitate the entry of new life into this world.

Being a participant in the joy experienced by the parents and family of newborns was simply thrilling for me. All of the delivery experiences I had previously been involved in were very upbeat and positive, with everyone generally leaving the labor and delivery room happy. This day promised to be no different. Mom and Dad were ecstatic as they awaited the birth of their first child.

Labor progressed without a hitch. As delivery approached, the doctor encouraged his patient to push. The excitement in the room continued to build as her water broke and the baby began emerging from the mother's bulging birth canal.

I recall the obstetrician encouraging her: "Come on, push as hard as you can, your baby is almost here!"

The baby began emerging breech or feet-first. As the torso was delivered, sight of the genitalia heralded a baby girl was about to be born. The excitement continued to crescendo until a few seconds later, the baby's head emerged.

A wave of cold, bone-chilling silence rippled through the delivery suite, stifling the excitement of the moment before. The newborn baby was anencephalic. This is a serious birth defect in which parts of the brain and skull are missing. Such a profound genetic defect is inconsistent with sustainable life.

The energy in the room morphed in a nanosecond from an atmosphere of palpable jubilation to one of a somber, sobering sadness with a deafening silence, broken only by the barely audible sobs of the newborn's horrified mother. In disbelief, the father helplessly looked to the physician for an explanation, knowing there would be none.

The baby had a frightening appearance, one that none of us had ever seen in our worst nightmare.

The doctor quickly handed the infant to the nurse, who winced as she was handed the deformed child. The mother chose not to hold the child, turning her head away as the baby was placed in a bassinet and whisked away.

The decision was made not to provide any sustenance to this newborn. Instead, nature would be allowed to take its course. No one expected the infant to survive more than a few hours. I recall the heart-wrenching conversations among the physicians, nurses, and the hospital chaplain. As there was no treatment for such a malady, it was the consensus of all involved in her care that any heroic measures would be fruitless.

At first I agreed with that assessment, but over the next several days, I was repeatedly drawn back to this child's bassinet that had since been tucked away in a small, dimmed cubicle in the far corner of the delivery suite.

I struggled. I struggled to find meaning in such a sad circumstance. What could be the purpose of such a roller coaster of emotions for these parents? I wondered why God would allow a fetus to be born, only to snatch away her opportunity of life so quickly?

Alone with her, holding her tiny hand and gently stroking her cheek, it was in this cocoon of love that insight first began trickling out from deep within me. I began sharing with this child how worthy she was of her time on Earth, explaining that it was her destiny to be here for however long she desired and that it was no mistake that her spirit had purposefully chosen the vessel she entered the world wearing.

Three days after her birth, without any fanfare, this gentle soul quietly departed her body. What she left behind for me was something very special—a new and different path of discovery. Her brief time on Earth and the evanescent crossing of our paths offered me glimpses of enlightenment as slowly and methodically, doors of understanding began to open for me.

I began pondering aspects of life that I had never previously considered. I questioned from where do we come and why?

In medical school I had been taught that our parents, unique creatures in their own right, combined their DNA with the primary purpose of offering us up as the generation to follow them. I came to appreciate that this perpetuating gene pool is how the Universe ensures its own immortality.

Many consider the day we were born as our birthday, the belief being that life begins with the first breath. Others embrace that life commences at fertilization when the strongest sperm wriggles its way into the egg's inner sanctum. Science has confirmed though that at the precise moment of what we generally define as conception, something already exists. Rather than an abrupt start to life with a smack on the rump, birth is offered as more of a continuation of life force that has forever been and forever will be.

From each contributor to fertilization, the merging of DNA results in a distinctive individual, a creation never before manifested. No two of us are exactly alike. Even identical twins are not identical. While they may appear to have the same physical attributes, each vessel we call a body is inhabited by a different soul, thus rendering them unique.

The flow of life force is the same for everything. There is no difference between the circulation of blood as it courses through a baby's arteries and the current of a trickling mountain stream. Such rejuvenating energy found in all things guarantees survival of everything and everyone.

Birth and rebirth are much like a cloud. It has always existed, though not necessarily in its present form. While it was once a droplet of rain falling from an overly saturated sky or manifested as a single crystal of ice, the cloud does not come from nothingness, nor does it ever cease to exist. It merely transforms again … and again … and again.

The purpose of the soul entering the body is to enable the evolution of the spirit. With each consecutive reincarnation, the goal is that each becoming will result in a more improved version of itself.

WHISPERS OF THE HEART:

1. Once you accept the flow of life force is the same for everything, you become one with the Universe. Swimming against the current can be arduous. Don't resist. Instead, go with the flow.
2. Try to remember when you first perceived the beginning of your current life. Birth and rebirth are much like a cloud that has always existed, though not necessarily in its present form.
3. Birth is no more a beginning than death is an ending. Both are an integral part of the natural order of our Universe.

CHAPTER 3
CIRCLE OF LIFE

Contemplate the image of a circle. It is one of the most universal shapes in the cosmos. Moons, as well as all the planets in our solar system, are visible in circular form. Not only are the organs of vision, our eyes, circular in shape, the eye of the soul, commonly referred to as the "third eye", the gate leading to spaces of higher consciousness in the Hindu religion, the Egyptian eye of Horus, and the All-Seeing Eye in Freemasonry also are observed by us to be in circular form.

Each day of our existence arises in circular fashion. As the Sun's nurturing radiance begins sharing its warmth, the shroud of darkness is gently peeled away. The Sun's brightness gradually intensifies as the hands of the clock approach high noon.

Pressing onward through the afternoon, diminishing in intensity as it goes, the Sun begins dimming toward evening once again as the circle completes itself and the day fades back into the darkness of night.

This cycle of darkness to light returning back again to darkness will partner with us every day and night of our precious time on this earth.

Nature and the seasons also unfold in a similar circular fashion. When winter arrives and all the vibrant colors of autumn fade into oblivion, the ground freezes and all foliage withers. The trees become bare as they let go of the attachment to their leaves.

As dead as everything appears to be, life still exists in the leafless cherry tree even though its blossoms and fruit cannot yet be seen. For as long as the environment remains insufficient for growth to occur, the tree will hover in hibernation. But when spring arrives and conditions become satisfactory for its resurgence, the tree's flowers and luscious cherries will manifest in all their delicious glory.

The same holds true for our life experiences. We may not initially appreciate the meaning offered by them until conditions are sufficiently ripe for our comprehension to blossom.

When winter melts into spring, nature as it always has, will come alive with the thaw as new growth emerges from rejuvenating slumber.

Summertime and its time of maximum sunlight and warmth return to us the blossoming of the full array of vivid colors and the expansion of luscious green foliage.

As summer begins to fade, the circle returns us to early autumn. Daylight hours steadily become shorter. Fall appears once again as the time to harvest the fruits of our labors. As late fall unfolds, desiccation of the plants occurs as they begin the process of returning vital elements to the soil in preparation for a new season of growth yet to come.

The process of aging has a circular aspect to it as well. Even if we take superb care of ourselves, time will incessantly chip away at us, wreaking havoc on our bodies and slowly adding more wrinkles to our faces while steadily depriving us of our hearing acuity and eyesight.

Old age is often referred to as the autumn of life because it is during this season that we finally get the opportunity to harvest the many accrued experiences that have enriched our souls.

The quietude of old age doesn't have to be a time of sadness.

In fact, one of the perks of aging is that it affords us more time to be still. Tranquility is a vital nutrient for the soul. As solitude settles on our formally hectic lives, this new downtick of activity can actually become a marvelous resource for our continuing development. Such downtime allows us to begin a process that leads us to a greater understanding of what we have become and where we are headed.

Instead of viewing the autumn of our lives as the degradation of our bodies, we should embrace it as a fruitful time of harvest for the soul. In this light, the process of aging can instead be a time of invigorating enlightenment during which we have the opportunity to re-examine all of the many potential lessons life has offered us over the years.

We have all been granted the gift of life, though the amount of time is uncertain. Too many of us make the mistake of judging life not by its depth but erroneously by its length based on linear time.

No matter how vigorously we protest, our stint in a particular incarnation is finite, a mere blink of the eye. In preparation for the next phase of life, we must not waste a moment of the opportunity.

WHISPERS OF THE HEART:

1. The circle of life has no beginning. It also has no end. It is continuous. Its unending nature always has been and forever will be. Don't fret the transitions. Embrace them!

2. When the time arrives, accept the autumn of your life. It is during this season that you'll finally get the opportunity to spend fruitful time in quiet introspection. Do you recall a time in life when chaos ruled? Do you remember when, out of desperation, you prayed for a more peace-filled life? Well, your time has arrived. You are deserving of the solace it offers.

CHAPTER 4

BORN TOWARD DYING

Our birth is nothing but our death begun.
~ Edward Young, *Night Thoughts*

Death is really a fallacy of thought. Cell by cell the physical aspect of each of us begins dying from the moment of conception. Each type of cell in our body has a different death cycle, its own timetable. The lifespan for cells comprising the stomach is a mere two days; for those lining the colon, three to four days. Skin cells regenerate every two to four weeks, red blood cells every four months, and some of the cells that make up bone can last up to 30 years!

Each year, humans lose and regain a mass of cells roughly equal to their own weight. Cells destroy themselves so that others cells might live. In doing so, they essentially commit suicide. During the process, their life force is introduced back into the environment where their energy is then used to revitalize the whole as new cells are generated to replace those that have served their purpose.

The process of cell death encompasses everything from the sloughing of the healthy lining from the uterus during menstruation to the formation of new synapses that permit the transmission of electrical impulses from one nerve cell to another. For every organism, the maintenance of its health is dependent upon this reliance on death. This is a statement worth repeating. *The maintenance of health is reliant on death.*

What makes a cell decide to commit suicide? The answer lies in the balance. Programmed cell death is critical to the destruction of cells that represent a threat to the integrity of the organism as a whole. The result provides us with a new body. Within this context, how could one ever consider death an enemy?

Every day we die many deaths. We are, in fact, different from moment to moment. In his book *Life After Death,* Deepak Chopra describes: "Every former self you have left behind is a ghost. Your thoughts, your body, your ideas have all changed. You have survived thousands of deaths every day as your old thoughts, your old cells, your old emotions, and even your old identity pass away. You are already living in the afterlife right now. What is there to fear?"[23]

What we refer to as death is but the beginning of yet another chapter in life. The challenge is that we must learn to accept dying while we are still alive. In doing so, death becomes not a failure but a triumph, with rebirth actually occurring well before we take our last breath.

"The day which we fear as our last is but the birthday of eternity."
~Lucius Annaeus Seneca

WHISPERS OF THE HEART:

1. Everyone experiences many little deaths. Rejoice in them while becoming revitalized with the life force that energizes all living things.

2. Remember that the maintenance of our health relies on death. Such a symbiotic relationship actually helps to sustain us.

   What we refer to as death is but the beginning of yet another chapter in this glorious journey called life. Change the thought about your demise. Anticipate with enthusiasm your next phase on the other side of life.

Part II:

Peeking Behind the Curtain

CHAPTER 5

LIFE IS A PASSING PARADE

*There is only one law in the universe that never changes—that is
that all things change and that all things are impermanent.*
~ Sogyal Rinpoche, *The Tibetan Book of Living and Dying*

Nothing stays the same. And yet, nothing is ever destroyed. The nature of the Universe is that everything is constantly undergoing transformation. At some point every single thing must change in order to allow the manifestation of what has been destined to come forth.

The apparent impermanence of life can be quite frightening.

Attempting to grasp something that by its nature is impermanent will prove as successful as attempting to clutch a handful of the viscous substance mercury. The more tightly it is squeezed, the less likely it is to be contained. The more strongly we hold on to the attachment and fail to acknowledge the impermanence of life, the more anxious our existence will likely become.

Life is a passing parade. As observers, some of us watch helplessly as the cavalcade of death continues on its unrelenting march threatening to overtake us. The awareness of our own mortality, false as it may be, is a constant reminder of the inevitable impermanence of life.

In *The Tibetan Book of Living and Dying*, Sogyal Rinpoche describes the heartbeat of death:

"There would be no chance at all of getting to know death if it happened only once. But fortunately, life is nothing but a continuing dance of birth and death, a dance of change. Every time I hear the rush of a mountain stream, or the waves crashing on the shore, or my own heartbeat, I hear the sound of impermanence. These changes, these small deaths, are our living links with death. They are death's pulses, death's heartbeat, prompting us to let go of all things we cling to."[24]

Contemplate the transience of nature. I was once the steward of a tall cactus plant given to me by my sister, Carole, horticulturist extraordinaire. One summer, over the course of several weeks, it began to sprout an appendage that grew a half an inch or so every day.

Late one night having been out with friends, I returned home around two a.m. As I walked past the cactus, I became aware that the appendage, now about eight inches long, had bloomed an exquisite flower with succulent white petals covered with beads of dew. The sweet fragrance it released was as delicious as it was beautiful.

Too exhausted to give it attention, I told myself that I'd enjoy it in the light of day. By the next morning though, the magnificent flower had withered, and the cactus had already begun letting go of the attachment to its now desiccating petals, several of which had already fallen to the ground.

My first thought was, *Awww, what a missed opportunity*! I lamented that this exquisite flower's impermanence had limited my enjoyment of it.

What I actually discovered over the course of time was that the transience of its beautiful bloom didn't negatively impact my delight of it in any way. In fact, my recollection of that early morning evanescent encounter with one of nature's awesome sensual offerings continues to occupy a beautiful memory in the recesses of my heart. The experience for me was not finite or limited in duration. In fact, from the perspective of this observer, the splendor of the observation remains alive to this day.

Sigmund Freud once took a sunny summer walk with an acquaintance. Freud's colleague made the glum observation that while nature is beautiful, its impermanence and the fact that its beauty was fated to become extinct once winter arrived caused him to feel no enjoyment of it. From his requiem *On Transience*, Freud offered this response to his friend:

> *"It is incomprehensible, I declare, that the thought of the transience of beauty should interfere with our joy in it. As regards the beauty of Nature, each time it is destroyed by winter it comes again next year, so that in relation to the length of our lives it can in fact be regarded as eternal."*[25]

Impermanence doesn't have to imply annihilation. I have often contemplated the antique furniture and paintings in our home. These pieces, lovingly chosen to enhance our living space, are precious beyond words or value to my wife and me. Each piece holds a special memory of how and where it was acquired. Many of our most prized possessions were purchased at garage sales, auctions, and the many estate sales we attended as we began the process of filling our home with gorgeous gems.

But after almost 50 years, I know there will come a time when Angela and I will, without regret, let go of our attachment to these timeless treasures. The essence of our home complemented by each of our cherished antiques will change as we decide to move on never looking back. Our abode will ultimately reveal its impermanence as the pieces of our mosaic we called home are sold off or given away.

As none of our children share our appreciation for antiques, I imagine when the time comes for us to downsize or when the last of us to survive in this material plane hits the dusty trail, our treasures, as they should be, will be offered up to the highest bidders who will begin creating cherished, albeit transient, memories of their own.

Like almost everything else, our bodies also have a limited shelf life. As we look in the mirror at ourselves, what do we see? We examine and then usually lament new wrinkles and blemishes that the aging process is bestowing on us. We all have our own literal or figurative "mirror, mirror on the wall." We primp and fluff and spray, adorning ourselves with ornaments and clothing in the hope of portraying a pleasing visage—one that, in reality, fosters a false façade of vitality.

But wherein lies the beauty? Is it what we see on the surface, or does the real beauty lie somewhere within the deep alcoves of our being?

Often when I find myself in a crowded place, I have the desire to become invisible so that I can observe without myself being observed. Recently I was traveling to Jamaica for a speaking engagement. I had a rather lengthy layover at the Atlanta airport. As I sat in the bustling terminal, what I observed as I looked out over the throng of travelers was that each person was adorned with a unique veneer. Some dressed impeccably while others like me were traveling in tattered Levi's. There were people of all races. Some were painted with heavy makeup; others had none. I saw a Buddhist monk dressed in a crimson and gold robe. Some of the people were old. A few were infants. Some were tattooed, and one lady had four nose rings. Not one of us looked alike.

In a waking meditative state, I scanned this microcosm of humanity without focusing on any of them individually. What I noticed once I got past the varied and individual trimmings each had applied to their physical vessel was the *essence* of each individual's soul. To my surprise, I observed an undeniable similarity in each of them, even though, at the same time, their exterior appearances differed. The observation confirmed in my mind the presence of the singular Divine found in each of us.

Two decades ago, the world witnessed the horrific destruction of the Twin Towers on 9/11. What remained of those once majestic and chiseled towers was rubble and unstable steel beams. Their veneer precariously leaned against their own mangled and twisted guts.

Who envisioned that they could so easily collapse to earth?

The truth is that all structures are unstable. Whether destroyed by crazed terrorists or as the result of natural disintegration, all forms are impermanent.

Having a penchant for cemeteries, I have slowly strolled through hundreds of such hallowed places. Intrigued by the stories of those long gone provides a level of serenity I don't experience anywhere else. As I stroll through the plots of these so-called final resting places, I invariably notice two distinct types of gravesites. One type is well attended, manicured, and might be adorned with flowers. It is obvious these plots are the repositories for individuals still remembered by someone. The other cemetery sites are of those long forgotten. Those cemetery graves are overgrown with weeds, are flowerless, and some of the tombstones are lying on the ground, broken and eroded, rendering the tombstone's message illegible. Those plots likely represent individuals of whom no one alive has any memory. Some remain the last vestige of all who had preceded them in life and death.

How does that happen, the forgetting of one's predecessors? It's no doubt a slow process as friends and relatives of the deceased join the multitude of those in the space of forgotten memories. But being forgotten isn't necessarily bad. From the second verse of the *Tao Te Ching*, Lao Tzu shares with us a timeless truth:

> *"The sage can act without effort*
> *and teach without words.*
> *Nurturing things without possessing them,*
> *he works, but not for rewards;*
> *he competes, but not for results.*
> *When the work is done, it is forgotten.*
> *That is why it lasts forever."*[26]

What is meant by these wise words is that one should live life, learning from the many lessons it has to offer. When the time comes for us to shed the skin of this existence, like a molting snake, we slough the mortal coil and reclaim our place in the marvelous oneness of the Universe. This is why when the work is done it is forgotten but lasts forever! The memory is what fades away in its impermanence.

WHILE WALKING THROUGH THE FOREST ONE DAY RECENTLY, I acknowledged that summer had run its course and was yielding to autumn. It became obvious that change was occurring.

A gust of wind blew through the canopy of trees above, and several dead leaves finally let go of their attachment to the trees. As they slowly drifted down, joining others on the forest's floor, the leaves spoke volumes to me.

We are surrounded by impermanence. Like everything, we must change as well. We are different from breath to breath. The river as it flows past us will never be the same river again. Nothing remains the same—ever. Yet, too often we resist change, holding on with a fervor that only fosters further suffering and turmoil.

In order for us to be at peace, change requires that we must let go. What we'll discover is that by letting go of the attachment, leaves lost today will be replaced by those that will sprout anew in the next spring. It is the way nature continues itself. If we can become ever mindful of the constancy of change, the cyclical harmony of life's impermanence will unfold, enriching our experience of life beyond our wildest expectation.

WHISPERS OF THE HEART:

1. When you learn to embrace the timeless truth that nothing remains the same, that everything changes including the physical you, then the natural flow of life and death will offer a peace and serenity never before experienced.

2. Learn to let go of the attachments to life, especially those aspects that have never served you well. From your spiritual perch, you will be able to experience life's beauty with much greater clarity.

3. We are different from breath to breath. Take a moment to be cognizant of the little comings and goings, the apparent births and deaths in your life. Do not fear such impermanence. Everything in this physical realm is impermanent, you included.

CHAPTER 6

EGO'S LAST STAND

How would you respond to the question: "Who are you?" Most of us would likely reply by describing our age, gender, job title and accomplishments, perhaps our marital status, ethnicity, or religion. But what if all those descriptors were to be stripped from you—could you still be?

We generally ascribe far too much importance on ego-driven pursuits. Ego is a person's sense of self-importance, a delusion of grandeur. It advances the notion that in order to be satisfied, fulfillment can only be found in material "stuff". Ego focuses far too much on acquisitions and physical appearance.

Pursuing such fictitious happiness by those whose lives have become monopolized by ego, promotes the constant yet insatiable urge to continue the rat race of acquiring even more of the trappings of success that we mistakenly believe fulfill us. Enslaved by such worldly pleasures, paradoxically, we are left emptier by our desire for more.

Ego and the body share something in common—they are both impermanent. Neither is present before birth nor found to be intact after death. For however long we remain on Earth, the body is a tool at our disposal. It is not something that we are.

The domicile we call the body has a simple purpose. It provides the vehicle through which our purposeful incarnation unfolds. Our spiritual advancement becomes manifest through our experiences with the body serving as the conduit through which we explore and acquire knowledge.

This is not meant to minimize the critical role played by the body; there is no question that it serves a vital function. In fact, every cell in the body is surrounded by millions of like-minded cells that become organized in the form of specifically functioning organs. Each cell possesses its own intelligence and has its own consciousness.

In order for the whole to survive, every cell must relinquish its individuality. Working in conjunction with many different types of cells, the goal is to benefit the whole.

When the time for transition arrives, our accrued intelligence withdraws from the mix. All of the cells that had symbiotically worked so well together lose the capacity to perform their designated tasks.

Even if we take superb care of our vessel, the body will eventually fail. When this occurs, the physical body will disintegrate. Each cell, dissolving into its essential components, will then transmute into different forms of energy that will remain in repose until such time as they will be called upon to reconvene with other elements that will join with other cells in new and unique combinations.

Intriguingly, at the moment of what we call death, all of this physical separation falls by the wayside as the soul loosens from the shackles of the human experience. The spirit is released from its vessel to reclaim its place in the cosmos.

While ego fears death and its finality, the soul has no such trepidation. Its connection is with the eternal aspect of space and time that promises there is no such thing as death.

Where the soul goes once separation has occurred may not be a distinct place but rather a different state of being. With this understanding, our loved ones who have crossed before us remain in close proximity. While they may be invisible to our gaze, our hearts easily recognize them.

The body is but a temporary abode. In the overall scheme of things, what happens to it is really immaterial. Its destined course is a product of nature; its survival is unimportant.

In letting go of ego, appreciation of our true nature begins to unfold as our spiritual core reawakens. What emerge are glimpses of insight, moments of inspiration.

In this more enlightened space, we will come to embrace that our inner being, our authentic self realizes that this world is not the final destination point. The earthly experience we all have is but a temporary stopover, a springboard on our unique journey back to the Creator of Everything.

WHISPERS OF THE HEART:

1. Look deeply inside those you encounter today. It is there you might catch a glimpse of their essence. Look past the facade of their physical form and trappings. Instead, find the Divine in them, recognizing it within you as well.

2. Your greatest teachers can be those who have few possessions and little ego.

3. Instead of **E**dging **G**od **O**ut, let go of ego. As you do so, your true nature will begin percolating to the surface, unfolding as your spiritual core reawakens.

CHAPTER 7

BEYOND THE THRESHOLD
OF FEAR

*Anxiety is a thin stream of fear trickling through the mind. If encouraged,
it cuts a channel into which all other thoughts are drained.*
~ Robert Albert Bloch

Several years ago, while experiencing a prolonged and very stress-ful time in my life, I received a phone call from my urologist. He informed me that my biopsies had come back positive for prostate cancer. My initial response to that shocking news was a feeling of chagrin. I felt like a little boy who had gotten caught with his hand in the cookie jar!

Similar to Lance Armstrong, who had to have known he'd eventually get caught in his lies, I also knew it was only a matter of time until the stress I had allowed to fester within would begin to devour me.

The effects of the stress had switched my immune system into the off position. Its malfunction allowed *dis-ease* to gain entry into my body in the form of cancer cells within my prostate gland, cells that began multiplying and expanding unimpeded by an ineffec-tive immune system.

Significant imbalance had accrued in my life. And now, to add to my list of worries, I got to add the isolation and fear of a pos-sible early demise. My soul had become smothered as I had allowed myself to become overpowered by the destructive nature of the perceived stressors of my life. They had wrapped themselves so tightly around me that I felt as if I was suffocating. By giving fear and turmoil credence, my unhappiness had steadily increased.

As Usman B. Asif, RT, once said: *"Fear is a darkroom where negatives develop."* Fear can be an overwhelming emotion resulting in significant mental agony. It can thwart the potential we have for happiness and security.

Most of our fears have irrational thought as their foundation. We hang on to things without even knowing for certain whether or not they are true. Fear isn't real—it's a fabrication of the mind, a story we tell ourselves that distorts reality.

It seems reasonable, however, that we might fear something that cannot be seen or comprehended. Imagine the terror that prehistoric man must have felt when he witnessed thunder and lightning, having no appreciation whatsoever of their nature.

Often, fear proliferates in our heads as we replay the perpetually looping narratives of past traumas or ruminate over yet-to-occur scenarios. Left unchecked, tentacles of fear can burrow deeply into our core, granting destructively negative energy undeserving strength.

One of the greatest trepidations many of us experience is the fear that when we die, we become nothing. Understandably, if we believe that we're born from nothing, then it is only logical to reason that when we die, we must return to the very same nothingness. For many, accepting this possibility is agonizing. Even for those steeped in their faith, death can be a terrifying prospect. I recall two of my patients, both of who were facing impending deaths. One was a minister, the other, a nun. What perplexed me was how spiritually unprepared they appeared to be despite the fact that their individual faiths promised them eternal life.

As we face death, many of us will enter unchartered and turbulent waters. Much of the turmoil stems from the insecurity of not knowing for sure what awaits us on the other side. Will our "heaven" be populated with those loved ones who transitioned before us, or are we doomed in death to perpetual isolation?

Not only might we experience fear of the unknown during the actual process of dying, but our apprehension might also include being fearful in anticipation of the physical pain and suffering that often partners death.

Many of us deal with our own looming death employing diversion and denial. In our attempt to escape the fear and loneliness death poses, we often thrust ourselves into an endless flurry of activity. Compulsively, we busy away our lives with mindless tasks that may prevent us from having to tackle important end-of-life considerations. Some of us will get blindsided, ending up hospitalized in critical condition, too weak at that point to address our imminent demise.

For those who spend the last days of life hooked up to mechanical devices such as ventilators, heart machines, IVs, and monitoring devices, the experience can be quite anxiety provoking and dehumanizing.

Not infrequently, the hospital staff objectivizes non-communicative patients. In part, this is a defense mechanism, a denial of sorts on the part of the medical and nursing staff, perhaps driven by their own uncomfortable feelings regarding death.

This impersonal approach to the individual doesn't necessarily interfere with the medical staff's ability to address the physical aspect of the patient's care, but ignoring the spiritual and emotional needs of the patient ignores what I believe to be the most important facet of care at this most important juncture in life.

It's easy to imagine how stressful and frustrating this must be for the person who has lost total control of his life. From the moment he arrives in the ER by ambulance, out of necessity for efficiency, the plan of care is dictated by the hospital's schedule and priorities, not those of the patient. As a rule, the patient is placed in anything but a nurturing environment often losing what little autonomy remains.

In defense of the above approach, there are times when decisions regarding emergent care must be made at the medical provider's discretion without the patient's consent.

One evening during my internal medicine training, an elderly woman arrived via squad to our emergency room. She was in extremis. Her breathing was labored and very shallow. I could tell that at any moment, she was about to stop breathing. With a life-threateningly low oxygen level in her bloodstream, time was of the essence; a decision needed to be made very quickly whether or not heroics should be initiated in an attempt to save her life.

Out in the ER waiting area, her next of kin, a priest, was awaiting word of her condition. After I explained to the priest the gravity of his aunt's situation, he pondered for just a second and offered that if all we could do was to bring her back to the same quality of life she had prior to this emergency, his belief was that she would refuse any heroics.

With that information, I rushed back into her room to inform the medical staff not to proceed with any heroics, only to find that she had stopped breathing shortly after I had left her room. She had been intubated and was now hooked up to a breathing machine.

I shared with the staff the next of kin's wishes for no heroics to be performed, and I instructed them to remove the tube from her airway so that we could allow nature to take its course.

One nurse in particular felt very strongly that to do what I had ordered would be "murdering" the patient, as she put it. Faced with a dilemma I had not previously encountered, I ultimately sought the advice of our hospital's legal counsel.

He asked me if she was alert. At this time, her oxygen level had returned to normal, and my assessment was that with the assistance of a ventilator, she had regained consciousness to the point that I was certain she was of sound mind and capable of making her wishes known.

His suggestion was that I ask the patient what, in fact, she wanted done. I was to ask her in two different ways whether or not she wished to remain on the ventilator. The first way I posed the question would require an affirmative answer from her; the second query, crafted differently, would require a negative response.

The fear in her eyes was obvious. In order to protect her from harming herself, both hands had been secured to the side rails of her gurney. She was desperate to get the tube removed from her throat. With each question, although agitated, she made it very clear by frantically nodding yes and no that she understood the gravity of her circumstance. There was no doubt in my mind that her responses were appropriate. She clearly indicated that she did not wish to be resuscitated, she wanted no heroics to be performed, and she wanted the tube in her lungs removed immediately!

With that information, I called the hospital lawyer who suggested that I document the encounter in the chart, and he informed me that he thought it would be permissible to remove the breathing tube from the patient.

Despite this knowledge of the patient's wishes and the corroboration of the patient's next of kin, several of the staff still felt morally obligated not to remove the tube.

After several very stressful phone calls back and forth between the hospital lawyer and myself, the decision was made in concert with all those involved, including her nephew, the priest, to leave the tube in her throat, to disconnect it from the ventilator, and transfer her to a regular floor where the inevitable terminal event would more than likely occur quickly.

A week later, I was walking down the hospital corridor when out of the corner of my eye I caught sight of something very strange. Seated in one of the hospital rooms reading Thoreau was the very lady I assumed had died! I couldn't believe my eyes.

I hesitantly entered her room, explaining to her who I was and what had transpired in the ER a week before. For a moment, I thought I saw a brief expression of fear on her face, but it passed quickly. I then asked her a question, the answer to which still blows my mind. The question I posed to her was what would she have wanted me to do in the very same scenario.

Her very stately response was: "Well, doctor, since I came to the hospital to be treated, I would assume that is exactly what you should do!"

I lost the wager on that one, folks. I would have bet the farm based on her answers to my questions in the ER that she would have wanted the exact opposite done for her. I guess that's why they call it the practice of medicine!

I encouraged her to document her wishes precisely with a living will to ensure that her preferences would be honored should she ever experience a similar emergency again. I encourage you, the reader, to do the same.

WHILE NAVIGATING THE DYING PROCESS, we will likely fear the loss of control. We may find it abhorrent having to rely on others to assist us with the most basic of requirements. No doubt we will dread the indignity that the physical ravages of our disease might impart upon us. Profound sadness will be endured over the imminent separation from loved ones and friends we hold most dear. But perhaps most of all, we'll lament losing the body that has carried us throughout our lives, the thing which we have relied upon the most to define who we are.

As we become filled with anxiety, we then attract into our lives the very thing we had hoped to avoid. Such paralyzing fear of death can rob us of what little pleasure still exists in life.

On occasion, our apprehensions are exacerbated by some religious leaders who have fueled such unsettling anxiety by warning us of horrific punishment that will be meted out after our death for sins we have committed.

Many of us try to avoid at all costs pain and suffering. But in truth, such anguish can be an invaluable tool. Rather than attempting to run away as fast as we can from the distress, we should instead strive to embrace the agony and torment as the great teachers they are.

If we succumb to the pain and sorrow, we'll end up becoming hostages to our fears instead of growing through them. The best way to approach the fear of death is to ask of it: *What am I to learn from you?*

"It is a bewildering thing in human life that the things that cause the greatest fear is the source of the greatest wisdom."

~ C.G. Jung[27]

IT'S INTRIGUING HOW SOMEONE YOU BELIEVE YOU ARE MENTORING ENDS UP MENTORING YOU. My sister's husband, Carl Lutnick, was such a person. He was a strong-willed, pragmatic man. If there are any words in the English language that defined the life of Carl, *perfect order* is what described it best. Carl possessed a marvelous ability to compartmentalize. He had a unique capacity to reduce complexity to simplicity, thereby placing everything in proper perspective, in *perfect order.* As a banker, orderliness was certainly an important attribute for him.

His life was seemingly in perfect order; everything was packaged neatly, placed on its own particular shelf. This is not to imply that Carl was obsessive-compulsive. He was, simply speaking, well organized. The perfect order in which he arranged his life also helped those around him arrange theirs.

Carl was diagnosed with advanced metastatic prostate cancer; he knew from the outset that his days were numbered. It came as no surprise that during his infirmity, Carl's life would continue to unfold with the same discipline that had worked so well for him up to that point. In that fashion, he was able to maintain perfect order even as he prepared to depart this life.

When I think of Carl, Jack LaLanne comes to my mind. For those of you old enough to remember, he was the original American fitness guru, a guy who set a world record of 1,033 push-ups in 23 minutes!

Carl exercised every other day of his life, embracing a workout ethic similar to that of LaLanne. The fruit of his labor gave Carl a chiseled physique, which embodied strength, not only in the physical sense but provided him with strength of mind as well. Jealous as we all were, Carl looked many years younger than his actual age.

When LaLanne turned 60, he successfully swam from Alcatraz Island to Fisherman's Wharf in San Francisco—while handcuffed. By the way, he was also shackled to a boat weighing over a thousand pounds!

This metaphor is marvelous. As we all swim through life, we can become overly encumbered by the baggage we drag behind us. If the weight is allowed to do so, the load will ultimately pull us under, torpedoing our efforts to stay afloat. It is not about how much the load weighs; it's all about how we carry it.

Carl was an inspiration to those of us blessed to be in his inner circle. He kept his terminal diagnosis to himself, continuing to go to the gym every other day.

Despite his fortitude and perseverance, I knew he was afraid of the unknown, of what might lie ahead for him. When the time was right, we talked openly about his fears. It was therapeutic for both of us.

As death began knocking louder at his door, Carl knew that he would need to muster what inner strength remained for the last leg of his life's journey. Of course, he made sure his finances were in order and that their home was in tip-top shape.

Carl contacted the local hospice organization and requested a meeting with its directing physician. Mind you, this was eight months before he would ultimately begin taking advantage of the many marvelous services they offered. At this point, he was still working out, and although he had lost some of his muscle mass, he looked remarkably healthy.

I recall the hospice physician commenting on Carl's healthy appearance, even expressing that he wished all of the people who could benefit from hospice would come in early enough to maximize the services hospice offered. Sadly, according to him, too many people wait until the final few days to get hospice involved.

Carl made his wishes known to the hospice physician. He made it clear what his expectations were when the time came that he could no longer care for himself. He also conveyed his desire not to have to experience the excruciating pain he anticipated would accompany him on the final part of his journey on Earth.

As the months unfolded, we all watched helplessly as Carl's disease ravaged his once-chiseled body. Relinquishing his workout sessions was likely the most difficult thing for him to do.

When the time came for hospice to complement his care, it was a seamless transition. All that he might need had been placed at the disposal of his caregivers. Everything Carl had requested was done for him exactly as he had been assured it would. For this man of strength who had always been in control, Carl was able, for once in his life, to rely on someone else to lean on and to ease his burden.

Hospice made sure that he experienced no anxiety and no fear. His pain and all of his other medical concerns were addressed in marvelous fashion. Up until his final hours with us, he remained alert but not in agony. My brother's final days were perfect—peaceful and filled with love.

Thanks to hospice, Carl's transition was made easy. All of his fears had been relieved. What better way to depart!

He took his last breath at three o'clock in the morning. Hospice was called, and within an hour, in the middle of the night, the nurse arrived along with several caregivers. They silently, unobtrusively, and respectfully went about their business. By the time they finished 45 minutes later, Carl's hospital bed and everything hospice had been using to assist him had been removed from the house, leaving our family to begin the process of grieving.

The key is to extricate fear from our thoughts. As Dr. Wayne Dyer related in his book *Change Your Thoughts–Change Your Life*, if we do not allow fear to gain entry into our consciousness, we can experience life while on the active side of infinity. We won't be encumbered by the limitations imposed by this worldly experience. "Through knowing yourself to be a spiritual being having only a temporary human experience, you can freely traverse this life being an observer, who can witness the end without ending."[28]

So, how do we extricate ourselves from the frozen shackles of fear? The answer lies in discovering ways to soften death's grip of terror on us. Once we do, we're actually able to enjoy the remaining events of our life as they unfold, difficult as they may be.

According to Christian doctrine, one shouldn't fear death, the vehicle in which one rides in order to reconvene with God. In verse 1 Corinthians 15:55, *"O death, where is your sting?"* Paul suggests that even though the sting of a bee causes pain, it can only sting once. And while the fear of the bee sting continues to be unnerving, the sting itself no longer wields any power. Only the fear of it does!

In the movie *Little Big Man*, the native American grandfather walks to his own funeral pyre and implores his grandson: "Do not be sad. Today is a good day for me to die."[29] Those who are enlightened don't fear death; they anticipate their demise with excitement and with innocent intrigue.

> *"The day which we fear as our last is but the birthday of eternity."*
> ~ Lucius Annaeus Seneca

WHISPERS OF THE HEART:

1. What can you do today to turn off the trepidations you have about your life? First, accept that fear isn't real; it's a fabrication of your mind. We tend to tell ourselves stories that distort reality. Fear proliferates as we replay the perpetually looping narratives of past traumas or fret over yet-to-occur scenarios. Change the thought. Only you control what you think. No one else wields that power!

2. Not only might we experience fear during the actual process of dying, but our apprehension might also include being fearful in anticipation of the physical pain and suffering that often partners with death. We seldom appreciate that the fear of suffering is often far worse than the actual suffering itself.

CHAPTER 8

A TASTE OF PARADISE

What if you slept?
And what if in your sleep you dreamed?
And what if in your dream, you went to heaven
And there plucked a strange and beautiful flower?
And what if when you awoke
You had the flower in your hand?
Ah, what then?
~ Samuel Taylor Coleridge

Near-death experiences (NDEs) have been described through-out recorded history. One of the earliest known reports was in Plato's Republic, written about 300 BC. In that story, a soldier who had sustained a fatal injury was revived. He described his transition into death as being guided by what he perceived to be angels who assisted him in ascending from the darkness, leading him to a place of peace and joy.

The American author Ernest Hemingway described his NDE, which occurred in 1918 while serving with the Allied Forces in Italy. A mortar shell exploded near him, badly wounding both of his legs. As he eased toward death, he described how it felt as his soul popped out of his body "like you'd pull a silk handkerchief out a pocket by one corner. It flew around and then came back and went in again and I wasn't dead anymore."[30]

Dr. Carl G. Jung described his NDE in this way after suffering a heart attack: "It seemed to me that I was high up in space. Far below I saw the globe of earth, bathed in a gloriously blue light... My field of vision did not include the whole earth, but its global shape was plainly distinguishable... The sight of the earth from this height was the most glorious thing I had ever seen... The images were so tremendous that I myself concluded that I was close to death. My nurse afterward told me, 'It was as if you were surrounded by a bright glow.' That was a phenomenon she had sometimes observed in the dying."[31]

Jung fervently believed that this experience was not the product of imagination or a "fevered brain." The visions, he was convinced, were real. "There was nothing subjective about them; they all had a quality of absolute objectivity."[32]

One of the most unique near-death experiences was described by Dannion Brinkley, author of *Saved By The Light*. At 25 years old, his "lively dance with death" occurred when he was struck by lightning during a fierce electrical storm. As a friend was frantically attempting to perform CPR, Dannion became a passive observer perched just under the ceiling. Everything he set his gaze upon, both animate and inanimate, vibrated with exquisite kaleidoscopic colors. For the first time in his life, he was able to see how everything was intricately connected.

After being pronounced dead in the ER and covered with a sheet as is often done to a deceased's corpse, Dannion found himself hovering above his body. He was surrounded by a shimmering bluish-gray energy that steadily drew him toward the opening of a swirling vortex where a brilliantly captivating glow beckoned him closer.

Soon he found himself standing within the light where he sensed an unequivocal feeling of all-consuming love. It was at this moment that a Being of extraordinary nurturing energy began to take shape. Dannion became focused on the presence of other souls in close proximity to him as the Being revealed a 360-degree panoramic life-review of his time on Earth. This review included everything he had ever said, everything he had ever done, and even each thought he'd ever contemplated.

By his own admission, Brinkley had led a despicable life, bullying and beating up anyone who dared to cross his path. The Being revealed to him each individual he had ever hurt and every victim he'd ever frightened. He was compelled to feel the same emotions experienced by each of the victims he had intimidated. For the first time in his life, he was forced to view his actions from the perspective of those he had terrorized.

After witnessing the hate and anger that had dominated his life, Brinkley was guided by the Being back to the realm of the physical world where he began facing the consequences of the very cruelty he had inflicted on others.

MOST INDIVIDUALS WHO HAVE HAD A NEAR-DEATH EXPERIENCE relate leaving their physical body behind. Often they hover over the bed or the place of their death, observing themselves from above.

My first experience with this sort of phenomenon was while working as a nursing attendant at an emergency room in Atlanta, Georgia. For several weeks, we had been on a roll of successful resuscitations. The past four days had brought six cardiac arrest victims to our ER. Despite the odds, all of them survived.

One evening, the doors to the ER flew open as paramedics barreled in pushing a gurney carrying a man who had gone into a full cardiac arrest. One emergency medical technician (EMT) was performing chest compressions from the patient's left side while another paramedic was squeezing an AMBU bag, a bellows placed over the man's nose and mouth delivering oxygen to the patient who was not breathing.

As he was lifted from the gurney onto the ER bed, our team exploded into action. Each of us had specific duties. Mine was to relieve the exhausted EMT who had been performing chest compressions for over twenty minutes. Standing on a step stool gave me greater leverage to use my upper body weight to deliver chest compressions forcibly enough to propel blood through his stilled heart. My position on the step stool also elevated me to a higher vantage point from which to observe the resuscitation attempt.

The telemetry monitor showed that our patient was in ventricular fibrillation, a chaotic heart rhythm disturbance that is incompatible with life. By definition, the man was actually dead before he rolled into our ER. Intravenous lines were inserted, and multiple rounds of medications were quickly administered. He also received numerous electric shocks to his heart from a defibrillator. Despite our efforts, none of this proved effective.

Every so often, the attending physician would instruct us to hold CPR. He'd observe for a moment, checking for any signs of life, feeling for a pulse, and when none was found, he'd order us to resume CPR.

After 45 minutes or so, the doctor in charge instructed us to halt any further resuscitation attempts. The patient was pronounced dead.

Less than a minute later, several of us noticed the patient blink his eyelids. This was despite the fact there was no heartbeat, and the man was not breathing. When this was brought to the attention of the attending physician, CPR was immediately resumed, an additional round of meds were given, and another shock was delivered to the patient's chest.

This time it worked! We excitedly watched over the next 5 minutes as his heart settled into a more stable rhythm. His blood pressure gradually returned to an acceptable level, and he began to breathe on his own.

I was still on the step stool, poised to resume chest compressions again if needed, when our "dead" patient's eyes fluttered and then slowly opened. He seemed to be looking beyond those of us in the room. But as he regained consciousness, his eyes began to focus on us as he spoke what I recall to be his first words: "I was up there in the corner of the room," he exclaimed, pointing upward. "I was hovering above you, watching y'all tryin' to save my life. I couldn't hear with my ears what you were saying to each other, but I heard you clearly in my mind. I was totally aware of everything around me. I could see, but it was in a totally different way than I have ever experienced vision before. It was like ... in a panoramic view. I could see everything all at the same time." Then he looked at each of us as he said, "You are so beautiful! Thank you, thank you."

That was my first encounter with someone having an NDE. It would not be the last. Little did I realize at the time, but the stage was being set for me to expand my awareness of something I had previously put little or no thought into. It would be over a decade until I would encounter the concept again.

MANY WHO SURVIVE AN NDE SEE A BRILLIANT LUMINOSITY at the end of a tunnel, described as a radiant glow of unconditional love. Margot Grey, a near-death researcher, described it this way: "As you are propelled forward, you anticipate reaching this light. Gradually as you travel toward it at an extreme speed, it gets larger and larger. As you draw nearer ... there is no sensation of an abrupt end of the tunnel, but rather more of a merging into the light. This light is not a light, but the absence of darkness. You don't look at the light, you *are* the light."[33]

Not everyone experiences the light. Some experience darkness, which can be quite frightening. One of my cardiac patients had undergone open-heart surgery. He was a profoundly religious man who had lived his life according to the template of his Savior.

Several days after he was transferred from the Cardiac Intensive Care Unit (CICU), I could tell something was deeply troubling him. After some coaxing, he hesitantly began sharing with me a terrifying incident he experienced while sedated and still hooked up to the ventilator in the CICU.

His recollection of the event was that "everything seemed to be going well." He perceived his heart was beating normally, running on all cylinders like a well-oiled engine. He could hear the steady clicking of his new heart valve. But suddenly, without warning, he felt everything stop. "I could feel the blood draining from me as I quickly lost consciousness."

He then looked up at me with an undeniable sadness in his gaze. He ashamedly shared his worst nightmare. "Terry," he said, "as you know, for many years, I have been a man steeped in my faith. I went into surgery with the resolve that having led a good and honorable life, I assumed that when it was my time to go, I would awaken in heaven."

The blind-sided shock for him was that his NDE was a profoundly dark one. He found himself in a place of utter misery. He described to me in vivid detail, the intense fear, gloom, and agony he felt. He went on to say: "It was like being sucked into the darkest black hole imaginable. I pleaded for help, crying out for God to save me. I implored God not to forsake me, begging Him not to abandon me in this torturous abyss."

He then described that after what felt like an "eternity in hell," he gradually started regaining consciousness, finding himself back in the CICU still hooked up to all of the machinery. He recalled slowly becoming aware of the steady "beep-beep-beep" of the monitor and the comforting "click-click…click-click" of his properly functioning new heart valve.

I was able to corroborate his account by reviewing his medical chart where I discovered that his heart had indeed stopped in the middle of the night. His blood pressure had plummeted, and a Code Blue had been called.

What had caused his heart to stop beating was a not-so-uncommon phenomenon that can occur soon after surgery of this sort. The circuitry of the heart becomes inflamed, blocking the transmission of the heart's electrical impulses. The result is asystole, or what is described in layman's terms as a flat line.

As a precaution for this potentially life-threatening event, temporary pacing wires are routinely sewn into the heart during surgery so that in the event the heart does stop, a temporary pacemaker can be turned on to save the patent's life. The charting of the event revealed that he was without a heartbeat for approximately 90 seconds. His "eternity in hell" had lasted by our linear measurements, a mere minute and a half!

Many of those who have NDEs, describe that once they reach the other side, they are met by their ancestors who accompany them on the remainder of their journey. Usually their peace and happiness are not verbalized but sensed in a way that is difficult for the person who experiences near-death to describe.

For most, a 360-degree panoramic view of their life unfolds. Similar to that experienced by Dannion Brinkley, many are able to observe not only their own life experiences, but to appreciate fully the implications their actions had on the lives of others. This places special emphasis on the ramifications of our actions, thus setting the stage for our karmic destiny.

In his book *Life at Death*, Dr. Kenneth Ring, a psychologist, concludes: "Both those who undergo a near-death experience and those who hear about them from others receive an intuitive sense of the transcendent aspect of creation."[34]

These individuals undergo a life-altering transformation, one that leaves them with a much clearer understanding of life and love. No longer fearing death and with newly discovered wisdom and knowledge, many return from the experience more fully appreciative of what is truly important in life.

Anita Moorjani, in describing her NDE in *Dying To Be Me,* shares:

Before my near-death experience, probably because of my culture, I used to think that the purpose of life was to attain nirvana—that is, to evolve beyond the reincarnation cycle of birth and death, striving never to come back into the physical.

But after my near-death experience, I feel differently. Even though I know I'll go on living beyond this plane, and I don't fear physical death anymore, I've lost my desire to be anywhere but the place I am now. Interestingly, I've become more grounded and focused on seeing the perfection of life in this moment, rather than focusing on the other realm.[35]

Like Moorjani, many survivors of an NDE find their interest in material wealth and their greed for possessions replaced by a thirst for a spiritual understanding they never before contemplated. Their NDE becomes life changing.

Of course, not everyone believes in NDEs. It has been the subject of extensive scrutiny by both theologians and philosophers, who have debated for millennia what happens when life as we know it comes to an end.

Even science has finally joined in the fray. The phenomenal progress brought forth by advances in medical technology has actually resulted in more individuals being successfully resuscitated. The irony is that many scientists remain resistant to the lessons they could learn from these near-death survivors. Until my personal awakening, I was one of those scientists oblivious to the possibility.

A great divide also exists among many religions on the topic of NDEs. As Erwin Lutzer states in *One Minute After You Die*: "We cannot overstate the deception perpetuated by the 'religion of the resuscitated' who report only the utopian idea that death leads to a higher degree of consciousness for all people regardless of their religion or beliefs."[36]

Skeptics will attempt to dispel credibility by ascribing NDEs to psychological and/or physiological afflictions. Others have suggested that chemical imbalances, medication-effect, and even wishful thinking and fantasizing are more logical explanations for these phenomena.

Indeed, the difficulty will likely forever lie in proving that NDEs actually do occur. In truth, we really won't know what happens to those who cross over, until it happens to us and we don't come back!

WHISPERS OF THE HEART:

1. Be open to the possibility that NDEs occur. Individuals who have undergone such a life-altering, transformative experience are generally left with a much clearer understanding of love. No longer fearful of death or dying, and with the wisdom and knowledge gained from such a profound occurrence, they return from the encounter more fully appreciative of life.

2. Take comfort in knowing that in order to become familiar with the road that lies ahead, we must learn from those who have come back.

PART III:

THE FACE OF DEATH

CHAPTER 9

LIVE LIKE YOU WERE DYING

Despite many major advancements in modern medicine, life still carries with it 100 percent mortality. Dying is something everyone will experience. How we navigate the process dictates what it is we are to become.

I recall hearing a story back in the early 1980s about two high school buddies who were roaming the Knobs of Kentucky hunting wild turkeys. Although the specifics of the events are hazy, here is my best recollection of them:

It was fall, and wet leaves covered the hilly terrain. As the duo hiked up a steep slope, one right behind the other, the second hunter slipped and lost his footing. Unfortunately, his shotgun's safety was not engaged, and as he fell to the ground, his Remington 870 discharged into the flank of his best friend.

The young man who had been shot was knocked forward to the ground by the impact of the 12-gauge shotgun slug. Feeling intense searing pain in his midsection, he looked down to see blood oozing from a gaping hole in his abdomen. Not knowing what had happened, the "fight or flight" response kicked in as he attempted to get up and run away. Less than ten steps from where he'd been shot, he collapsed. Suffering from extensive blood loss, his body rapidly began going into shock. Approaching a comatose state, his last thought was: *God, please don't let me die.* Then there was darkness.

The young hunter had suffered extensive damage to his internal abdominal organs and he had lost a near-fatal amount of blood.

He was rushed into emergency surgery. After ten hours in the operating suite with a team of three superb trauma surgeons and their associates, the young man was transferred to the Surgical Intensive Care Unit where he remained in critical condition, barely holding on to life. He had lost his spleen, part of his liver, and was left with a colostomy. It would be the first of many operations this young man would endure.

He remained hospitalized in the Intensive Care Unit of the trauma hospital for over three months. Several complications arose, the most serious being a condition known as DIC, or disseminated intravascular coagulation, a life-threatening bleeding disorder requiring multiple transfusions of blood and blood products. He received over 40 units of blood and nearly as many units of platelets.

Once stabilized, he was transferred to a rehabilitation facility where he underwent extensive physical and occupational rehabilitation. Ultimately, his colostomy was reversed, and he returned home to his family's farm six months after he was injured.

Having been told he would never be the same again, he set the lofty goal of returning to high school and playing football his senior year. Although he missed a year of school, it was with incredible tenacity that he was able to achieve his objective. Even though he wasn't able to make the starting lineup, it didn't matter to him. He had made the team.

Despite the terrible detour his life had taken, a circuitous course correction allowed him to get back on track. Off to college he went with his high school sweetheart. With plans to get married once they graduated from college, the two lovebirds intended to live happily ever after.

One would think surviving such an ordeal would be enough for a young man to endure, but life doesn't always take the direction we desire. Two years into college, his life back to normal, he received a devastating correspondence from the Centers for Disease Control. He was informed that extensive testing on some of the blood transfusions he had received while hospitalized were found to have been tainted with a recently discovered virus called HIV.

Now, back in the 1980s, being infected with HIV/AIDS was a death sentence. Little was known about AIDS at the time, and after frantic visits with several specialists in the field, he was told at best he had two years to live.

At the age of twenty, through no fault of his own, this young man whose life had held so much promise was now facing his own mortality again.

In the earliest days of public awareness, fear of the AIDS virus was widespread. Contracting the dreaded disease dealt the unfortunate recipient a fate almost worse than the plague itself. The reactions of his friends, some of his family, and even the love of his life, his high school sweetheart, were the same. Fearful of catching the deadly virus, they all banished him from their lives. The only person who was unwavering in his continued support was the friend who had accidently shot him in the back.

Forced into the isolation of what amounted to worse than a modern-day leper colony, his reaction was to escape the hell in which he found himself by drowning his sorrows in a bottle. He soon became an alcoholic, consuming over a fifth of bourbon daily.

When alcohol failed to sufficiently numb him, he entered the rabbit hole of crack cocaine, a new concoction of a terrible drug. It wasn't long before he became addicted, destitute, and homeless. To support his habit, he resorted to stealing from friends and family, his parents included. The few who had been supportive soon abandoned their tenuous relationships with him.

Five years later…

One morning after a weeklong binge of excessive drugs and booze, he awoke lying face down in a filthy ditch. He was covered in his own vomit and urine. Feces were caked to his clothes. Sluggishly rolling over on his back, his gaze took him from the disgusting image of being smeared in his own excrement to peering upward at a gloriously clear blue sky above.

From his vantage point on the filthy pavement, he began to reflect on his life. It was at this precise moment that he came to an epiphany. He had been given the AIDS death sentence over half a decade ago. *What have I done since?* He pondered. *I've squandered the past five years dying when I should've spent them living!*

Instead of fully appreciating the present moment, this young man realized he had been wasting his precious energy and whatever time he had left regretting the past and foolishly fretting about the dismal future he envisioned for himself. He had become so distraught by what appeared to be the overwhelmingly tragic circumstances of his existence that he lost all appreciation for life itself.

In his awakening, he came to embrace the notion that the now was the only thing guaranteed to him. It was the one thing that truly existed, his only reality. He came to realize that everything else on either side of the now—was delusion.

Within his immeasurable suffering, he found peace in something as simple as a singular moment of being totally present. And with his newly discovered solace, he was forever changed.

THE DAWNING OF A NEW DAY several years back brought with it profound sadness for me. Diesel, the 24/7 companion and best bud of our son, Tyler, was approaching the final moments of his life. Our handsome, eight-year-old Rottweiler had been recently diagnosed with bone cancer. From the outset, we were told his prognosis was extremely poor and that if he survived three months, it would likely be horrifically painful.

When I first opened my eyes that morning, I noticed that my wife, Angela, wasn't in bed next to me. I found her asleep on the kitchen floor, lying next to Diesel. A protective arm was wrapped around him. It was the first time in far too long I had seen this gentle giant not in pain.

I encouraged Angela to go upstairs to bed, assuring her that I would take over caring for our ailing friend. As I contemplated what Diesel had meant to us the past eight years, I acknowledged that only when we live our lives in service for others do our lives become worthwhile.

Diesel had indeed been a valiant servant, not only for Tyler, but for the rest of the Gordon gang as well. Intersecting our lives at just the right moment, he joined us a year before the automobile accident that left our son quadriplegic.

In the early days of his life-altering spinal cord injury, Tyler had been filled with overwhelming sadness. In the midst of his darkest despair, we held out hope that once reunited with his best friend, Diesel, Tyler's outlook on life might improve.

With much anticipation, we arranged for Diesel to be brought to Craig Hospital in Denver, Colorado, where Tyler was undergoing rehabilitation. When the day came for the reunion, we were all praying Diesel would be able to discover within our son the one thing no one else had been able to awaken in him—the will to persevere.

When an individual sustains a spinal cord injury such as Tyler's, the ability to sweat is lost. What we failed to take into consideration was that because Tyler didn't perspire, he no longer carried the unique, identifiable scent so well known to Diesel.

Diesel approached Tyler, who was sitting in his wheelchair. Inquisitively he sniffed around Ty for a few moments, then, not finding a recognizable smell, turned away. Tyler's anguish was palpable. A look of something that extended so far beyond disappointment slowly crossed our son's face. We were all devastated. *The* one thing that could have helped Tyler in his time of need was his companion, who turned away from him as if he were a total stranger.

It would be months later after our return home to Ohio that the two would finally reunite in a bond that became even stronger than before Tyler's accident. It was from the place of their conjoining souls that Diesel became not only an integral part of Tyler's recovery but also served as the central core of Ty's healing.

The two companions spent every day for seven years with one another. A dog is man's best friend. But I think the opposite is true as well. A man is a dog's best friend. This made Diesel's illness and impending departure all the more painful and unsettling. It just wasn't fair!

Those of you who are familiar with my first book, *No Storm Lasts Forever: Transforming Suffering Into Insight,* have read my thoughts on adversity and its purpose. On many occasions I have shared my truth that everything unfolds in perfect order, that life isn't unfair—it's always fair. When I have uttered those words in the past, I meant them. But with Diesel's impending passing, I must admit, my resolve was tested.

While in a steady state with life unfolding smoothly, it's easier to take a leap of faith and embrace a profound premise such as "life is always fair." But in times of heart-wrenching distress when life begins caving in, one's faith can be tested to the core.

Why do bad things happen to good people? In Tyler's case, I found myself asking: *God, hasn't my son suffered enough? Why this? What can Tyler possibly learn from losing his best friend at such a critical stage of his journey?*

I have discovered through enduring the pain and turmoil of our son's life-altering spinal cord injury that while the storms in one's life have the potential to create incapacitating turbulence in the mind, they don't have to.

Instead of viewing the death of part of Tyler's body as one of the most tragic things ever to happen to him, I came to accept it as a gift. Rather than bemoaning the experience and dreading its painful aspects, I decided to use whatever crossed my path as fodder for growth.

We have a choice. Resist the gift and become a victim who suffers, or choose to accept the gift and learn every single thing it has to offer.

We all lament the heartache in our lives, somehow feeling like we don't deserve the pain and suffering. Some consider the diagnosis of a terminal illness to represent a fall from grace. Because we have sinned, suffering is our payback. I believe the opposite, that disease and what accompanies it are actually a fall *into* grace. I have come to embrace that important lessons lie hidden within our painful experiences. We don't go through these agonizing encounters because we're bad people. And no, we're not being punished.

From John 9:1-3:

> *"As he went along, he saw a man blind from birth.*
> *His disciples asked him, "Rabbi, who sinned, this*
> *man or his parents, that he was born blind?"*
> *"Neither this man nor his parents sinned," said Jesus, "but this*
> *happened so that the works of God might be displayed in him."*

There are times in life when we've all asked ourselves: *Why me? Why do bad things like this keep happening to me?* The truth is, we are deserving of our heartache. We are worthy of the lessons God is giving us. It's all in changing the thought. The gift of each seemingly negative experience, if we choose to accept it, is a tool that helps to propel us onto a higher path. If in enduring such a circumstance, we fail to learn from it, *that's* the tragedy.

I sensed Diesel drifting away. The time had come to put on some peaceful music. Purposely, I didn't veer too far from him. He was too weak to move anything but his large expression-filled brown eyes that followed me around the room. Even in his weakened state, his eyes spoke volumes. I perceived they were thanking me for taking such good care of him.

I realized that I was projecting sad energy his way; I knew it wasn't fair for me to do that to our faithful servant during what was likely his last few hours with us.

I knelt next to him, gently massaging his neck. The sadness I had been wallowing in slowly morphed into a blessing for me. This quiet time with him gave me the opportunity to convey my deepest-felt gratitude for his loving service to our son. I shared with Diesel what a marvelous job he had done and how sweetly he had touched each of our lives.

I imagined that Diesel likely was thinking, *I can't leave yet. There's so much more for me to do!* It was during this silent conversation my soul was having with Diesel's that I realized I needed to help him concentrate not on tasks left undone but on his many successful missions accomplished.

Striving to create the most peaceful atmosphere possible for Diesel, I knew that too much grieving could evoke negative feelings in his heart. He might not be able to let go of the attachment to those of us grieving, which would likely prevent him from progressing on his destined journey to Eternity.

Diesel's time to transition had come. I could see through my tear-filled eyes that this beautiful creature understood and was ready for the next part of his journey. He was at peace.

His veterinarian, Dr. Kim Smith, had graciously offered to come to our home to help Diesel transition. Dr. Kim is much more than a vet. She's an angel. The loving care she gave to our Diesel made the experience all the more comforting.

With a cleansing final sigh, content with his life, our beloved friend transitioned to the other side of life.

In Diesel's dying, I learned powerful lessons. Much like what I sensed he might be contemplating as he approached the final moments of his life, many people in the midst of dying have similar feelings of disappointment and guilt. As the end draws nearer, they become filled with remorse about having inflicted pain on others.

From Tolstoy's *The Death of Ivan Ilyich*, a middle-aged arrogant bureaucrat is on his deathbed suffering a horrifically painful death. For his entire life, he has treated those around him with disdain, narcissistic condescension, and indifference. The closer he gets to death, the more he realizes how badly he has lived. And now, he is dying badly as well.

Two scenarios might have arisen from such a setting. In one, Ivan Ilyich might look up at his wife and ask, "What if my whole life has been wrong?" And then he dies without an answer. Can you imagine how devastating it would be, knowing your entire life had been a mistake?

An alternative scenario might just as easily unfold. Even though he's on his deathbed, Ivan Ilyich discovers that it's not too late. Despite the fact that he is rapidly approaching his last breath, there is still time to change. Time remains to begin living compassionately with love for those who have been and continue to be there to assist him. He becomes remorseful for the suffering he has caused. Through his metamorphosis, he ends up not dying in pain but immersed in the joy of love and compassion.

The lesson from Ivan Ilyich is that when we find ourselves at death's door, we shouldn't waste what precious time we have remaining by dying with remorse. Instead, we should strive to make amends for all of our transgressions. As caregivers, our goal should be to help minimize such destructive thoughts by encouraging the dying to concentrate instead on things done well in life.

We must be ever mindful that nothing taints the last days of a dying person's life more than being surrounded by falseness. Not honestly addressing the truth that the process of dying is unfolding risks further ostracizing the person who is transitioning. Failing to acknowledge the elephant in the room fosters further feelings of abandonment. The dying person might actually surprise us by yearning to talk about what she is experiencing. As difficult as it might be to discuss, strive to be open and honest.

IT WAS CLOSE TO THE END OF HIS VALIANT STRUGGLE WITH PROSTATE CANCER. My father, only 53 years old, was wasting away before our eyes. He had endured horrific, dehumanizing pain. This was a time before the advent of hospice and palliative care, when pain and suffering were not well managed at all.

Dad was no dummy. He knew he was dying, and so did the rest of us. He had observed the steady decline of his already-frail body.

While in the sterile environment of the hospital, he would softly groan whenever a phlebotomist would arrive at his bedside for yet another blood test ordered by one of his physicians. He sensed what was up when everyone was vague when he inquired about the results of the tests.

One of the observations that bothered me the most was as his treatment became more ineffective, his physicians spent less time with him.

The Hippocratic Oath that each physician swears to uphold mandates that we use appropriate treatment to help the sick according to our ability and judgment and, above all else, that we do no harm.

All too often, when physicians run out of viable options for treatment, they view death as a failure. What I noticed early in my career as a physician mirrored what I had observed in my father's physicians. They distanced themselves from the patient whose medical treatment had failed. The doctors' visits with Dad became shorter and shorter. I even noticed some wouldn't take more than a few steps into the room. The healing touch had evacuated the premises at a time when their patient needed it the most. There were some days when none of his physicians included him in their rounds at all. I think that was the most terrifying time for Dad.

Through negative reinforcement, I learned the importance of touching the dying. Often in the hospital environment, patients feel objectivized. They long for the human touch. They ache to be considered more than their disease.

At the time, I didn't understand the ramification of such a subtle abandonment. I must admit, I was quite frustrated. It would be years later that I came to understand they weren't bad doctors; they just didn't know how to care in a meaningful and empathetic way for their patient who was dying.

As the time drew nearer, Dad knew. He could tell it in the forced levity of his family's demeanor. He knew when he'd look into our eyes and saw them bloodshot from crying. He could see it on our mother's exhausted face.

Despite my parents' many hours alone together, I don't believe Mom and Dad ever had the type of conversation they both likely longed for but didn't know how to initiate. I am certain that from my father's perspective, he thought by not addressing the obvious, he was protecting his loving spouse.

My turn came one afternoon when it was just the two of us in his hospital room. I remember Dad saying to me, "Son, I'm not going to make it."

I recall offering an anemic response: "Oh yes you are, Dad. You're gonna get better. You can beat this. I know you can." I had to admit the inflection of my voice wasn't very convincing.

He knew I was not being truthful; I knew the same. One of my greatest regrets in life is that I didn't have it in me to address my father's fears head-on with him at a time when I suspect he needed me the most.

For the longest time after his death, I had a recurrent dream. Actually, it was more of a nightmare. Dad had moved away by himself while the rest of us continued living our lives. We knew he was out there somewhere, yet our lives carried on without him nonetheless. On occasion, our family would gather with him at his modest, meagerly furnished one-bedroom apartment. He seemed content with his circumstance.

Every time we'd visit him, which wasn't very often, we were all surprised that he was still alive! After all, his doctors had told us he wouldn't survive very long.

Self-psychoanalysis tells me that the nightmare I continue to have, even though now only rarely, represents the guilt I feel having not been open and honest enough to help my father in his time of greatest need. By not being forthright about his poor prognosis, I felt like I had ostracized him further into isolation, leaving him feeling abandoned, wallowing alone in his despair.

I was shocked to learn years later that my sister, Ronna, had felt similar guilt and had the same recurrent nightmare I had been experiencing.

I have since come to appreciate the metaphor of Dad's "moving away." His departure was, in truth, not that at all. While our lives continue to unfold as they should, his energy remains out there, available to us whenever we feel the need to connect.

Over the years, it turned out that this inadequacy on my part proved to be an invaluable instructor, teaching me the importance of open communication between the dying patient and his or her family. I was able to encourage many of the dying patients I treated throughout my career to talk frankly with their families and loved ones about their impending demise.

As it would be, the pain and agony I suffered with my father's dying helped me to become a more complete healer who was able to touch many hearts in ways I never imagined.

One of the most healing things we can do with our dying loved one is to profess our love for each other. My father was not a particularly demonstrative man. He grew up in the era where men didn't openly express their emotions. Even though I cannot remember him ever telling me that he loved me, there was never a doubt in my mind that he did. His actions spoke volumes when it came to my understanding of his loving but reserved nature.

The last time I saw my father, he was about to undergo a major operation that promised to ease the unremitting pain metastatic cancer had leveled upon him. He was lying on a hospital gurney, a surgical cap placed on his head. Just before being transported to the pre-surgical area, he paused and looked at each of us and slowly said, "I love you, Bev. I love you, Carole. I love you, Terry. I love you, Ronna. I love you, Andy."

His individual expression of devotion for each of us was impactful. I know for me those four words, "I love you, Terry," took on a whole new dimension as that was the last time I would hear my father's voice. He didn't survive the operation, but his last utterance to me taught me an invaluable lesson: *Always let people know how you feel about them.* There is not a day that goes by that I don't share with my wife, kids, and dear friends how very much I love each of them. Sadly, many like my father, wait until their terminal event looms over them before deciding to express their feelings. Even more tragic, some never reach that space of being able to express their love.

If we can succeed in the practice of dying while still alive, then one day, when we have learned all there is to know about life and death, we will without hesitation, let go of whatever remaining attachments are holding us back. And in that moment, we will become free.

The best way to achieve such liberation at the moment of death is through active preparation during life.

"There are so many little things, that it doesn't matter which of them is death." ~ Kenneth Patchen[37]

Occasionally, we take our time dying so that others might benefit and grow from our experience. For my family, it was a double-edged sword as my father faced the end of his life. Dad lived for an excruciatingly painful four years after his initial diagnosis. The time we had with him, sad as it was, gave us the marvelous opportunity to show our father how we truly felt about him.

In contrast, I recall being called to the emergency room one afternoon soon after beginning my medical career. A middle-aged man had been involved in an automobile accident. A truck had crossed left of center on the interstate and struck his car head-on.

His breastbone had been fractured, and as a result, he could barely breathe. He had a flail chest, a life-threatening injury where the sternum and ribs on the front of the chest are all detached from the rest of the chest wall.

As I attempted to place a breathing tube into his airway to help his labored breathing, he kept pushing it away from his mouth. He was intent on conveying to me perhaps the most important message of his life. He was begging me to be sure to tell his wife and son how much he loved them. He knew he was about to die.

While attending to him, I had a flashback to the morning of my father's death. Unlike my dad, this father and husband would not get the opportunity to say farewell face-to-face with his loved ones.

Navigating the experience of my father's slow demise, those around him got the chance to observe his reactions to each setback, each hurdle, and some rare successes. This gave those of us remaining behind a chance to learn valuable lessons from him. We all remember much about how he lived, but perhaps more importantly, we'll never forget the strength and fortitude in how he faced his death.

His acceptance and the dignity he demonstrated through his infirmity were life-changers for our family.

I HAVE LEARNED OVER THE YEARS THAT DYING DOESN'T HAVE TO BE SAD. Humor is more than okay when it comes to interacting with the dying. It may actually help alleviate considerable pain and agony.

Norman Cousins, editor of the *Saturday Review* magazine, suffered from what was ultimately diagnosed as a fatal connective tissue illness. As he navigated through the experience of his own infirmity, he became interested in the role emotions played in combating disease. While hospitalized, he began watching movies that caused him to laugh out loud. Surprisingly, he discovered that the comedies gave him remarkable relief from the excruciating pain that had not been eased by heavy doses of very strong pain medications.

Some physicians have discovered a secret to healing the body and the spirit. They have found a special potion called laughter, which releases endorphins, naturally occurring morphine-like substances into the brain, causing the body to relax while strengthening the immune system.

Some significantly profound people are humorous because they see more than what is obvious to others. Dr. Hunter "Patch" Adams is one such physician. He has taught us that humor can be therapeutic. If you haven't seen the movie *Patch Adams*, you must. It's based on Patch Adams' life story and his book, *Gesundheit!: Bringing Good Health to You, the Medical System, and Society through Physician Service, Complementary Therapies, Humor, and Joy.*

In the movie, he asks an angry man who is dying of pancreatic cancer if it would be okay to ask his wife out on a date after he dies. After a moment of disbelief crosses the man's face, the patient doubles over, howling in uncontrollable laughter.

Patch and his dying patient were able to connect and share a dimension of consciousness of which many others are not even aware. While most would likely feel very uncomfortable being jovial while talking with a dying person, I believe people feel important when someone cares enough to make them laugh.

One of the nicest compliments ever paid to me was when one of my patients told me I reminded him of Hawkeye Pierce from the TV show, *M.A.S.H.*

Now, some physicians might be offended by such a comparison, but I was flattered to be described in such a way. You see, Hawkeye Pierce was a jokester; he always had a wisecrack, a quip on the tip of his tongue. He was constantly concocting some sort of tomfoolery to play on his friends, fellow co-workers, and even on those who outranked him.

The beauty of the man was that in a nanosecond, when the need arose, he became a serious healer. In an instant, he could morph into a superb surgeon who became hyper-focused and could operate with the best of them as he saved the lives of injured soldiers.

Hawkeye and Patch Adams had somehow learned how to heal not only with their gifted hands but with their hearts as well. They knew that laughter could be beneficial, cheap medicine.

Dying shouldn't be bogged down in sadness. If the act of dying is viewed not as a threat but as an opportunity for growth, we can come to appreciate it as a transitioning event of beauty and continuation. We can then be free to experience it without sorrow, savoring it with delight and even humor.

THIS BOOK YOU ARE READING, *No Beginning... No End,* has been writing me for many years. Over the course of its 20-year history of coming to fruition, there have been some very special souls who have crossed my path. One of those stewards of Light was Chuck Collins.

Chuck and I shared several things in common. We both enjoyed writing; he authored several novels in a series called *The Radio Murders.* I had just completed my first novel, *My Heart Will Go On and On.* Chuck and I also shared a fascination with the unknown. We also shared many good laughs together!

After multiple attempts to meet in person, Chuck and I finally set a date on the calendar. When he arrived at our home, we were both pumped, anxious to dive into this new friendship to see where it would take us.

As we began our conversation seated outside overlooking our lake on a gloriously sunny spring day, Chuck hesitantly asked me if I'd mind if he asked me a medical question.

He shared with me some very disturbing symptoms he'd been experiencing. After listening to his description, I suggested that he see a physician immediately and arranged for him to do so that very afternoon.

Our initial get-together had taken us in a direction neither had anticipated. In the next several weeks, Chuck was diagnosed with a glioblastoma, a malignant brain tumor. One of the things that had brought us together, our interest in the unknown, now became intertwined with an aggressively growing mass in this beautiful man's brain.

Over the next two years, I would be blessed to share a circuitous journey with my dear friend, one that would take him from being a healthy and vibrant energy force to a place where he faced the robbing of his brilliant mind.

The many conversations we shared through the course of his infirmity were exquisitely insightful. Nothing was left off the table. We talked about his deepest-held fears—about mine too. We shared our feelings on the hereafter and where that might be. Chuck Collins became my mentor.

He endured months of treatment that included many rounds of chemotherapy, gamma knife radiation, and three operations on his brain.

One morning, immersed in one of our many deep discussions about life and death, Chuck posed one of the most profound questions I have ever contemplated. He asked, "Terry, why do you suppose I am *not* going to die today?"

For the time being, I am going to leave you with that thought to ponder. I trust a greater understanding of such a concept will unfold as together we continue on this journey toward enlightenment.

WHISPERS OF THE HEART:

1. As you begin each day, contemplate the fragility of life and how its tenuousness might encourage you to live your remaining life more fully. Talk about being spiritually liberated!

2. If you are blessed enough to be with someone who is near death, become a good listener. Demonstrate unconditional love with no judgment attached. It is an honor to share such a sacred place with one who is about to transition.

3. Create the most peaceful atmosphere possible surrounding the dying individual, as too much grieving evokes negative feelings in the heart of the dying.

4. Imagine what an impact it would make if you looked into the mirror of death and began living like you were dying.

CHAPTER 10

WHEN LOVE AND DEATH EMBRACE

From the moment of our entry into this world, a connectedness with others occurs. Some of these links last a short time, while others endure a lifetime or longer.

Perhaps you're old enough to remember as a youngster going to the carnival that came to town once a year. I recall an exhilarating ride with cars propelled by electricity delivered from a pole that reached up to the ceiling. Each car had a steering wheel and an acceleration pedal. With sparks flying off the ceiling, the cars glided on a smooth surface sprinkled with graphite to decrease friction. The object of the carnival ride was to bump into other cars, knocking them off course, hence, the name "Bumper Cars."

We who are temporary travelers on this earthly plane are like bumper cars. On occasion, we bump into another car, and the force of the collision causes both to be repelled in opposite directions from one another. At other times, a gentle tangential impact with another bumper car nudges both vehicles onto a parallel path with one another.

The truth is our journey through life is really a solitary one. That's not meant to imply that we are alone. The Creator of Everything is forever conjoined with us every step of the way. But even though we may become aligned with others, be it for a few days or many years, everyone's voyage is in fact, a unique experience. No one but me is privy to my every thought. No one else can understand everything there is to know about me. No one sees what I see or shares the same exact perspective I do.

Have you ever wondered where a lifetime of love goes when we die? Does all the love we accrue simply waft away at the moment of death like an extinguished candle?

There is no doubt that the capacity to love is an integral part of the human experience. The brain has been given the esteemed title of command center of the body, integrating most of the bodily functions required to maintain viability.

There are those who believe love, being an emotional phenomenon, is generated in the mind, which is housed somewhere within the brain tissue. If this is so, why do the feelings of love and for that matter the pain of grief seem to emanate from the area in our chest where the heart resides?

Recently, science has discovered that the heart has its own extremely complex nervous system that enables it to function independently of the brain. This research has confirmed the heart is much more than just a pump. It possesses its own circuitry consisting of more than 40,000 neurons capable of detecting things such as circulating hormones and neurochemicals that drive electrical impulses. This functional "heart brain," as coined by neurocardiologist Dr. J. Andrew Armour, has been shown to influence not only the heart but to impact some brain function as well. The heart is also believed to oversee many of the bodily functions previously ascribed to the command center in the brain. In other words, the heart with its own intrinsic nervous system has a mind of its own!

Paul P. Pearsall, PhD, is a psychoneuroimmunologist and author of a study titled, "Changes in Heart Transplant Recipients that Parallel the Personalities of Their Donors."[38] In researching heart transplant recipients, he and his co-authors found that living tissue from an organ donor maintains a memory that can be transferred at the cellular level to the person receiving the organ. As preposterous as it may sound, love just might be one of the many components of that transferred memory!

The question then becomes: wherein lies the memory? If love resides within the heart, is its memory lost when the heart is removed? Is it possible to lose the love a heart has spent a lifetime accumulating?

Where does love reside—in the transplant donor or the recipient? The answer rests in the fact that cells, which have been continually imprinted by a heart, retain their memory. When a transplanted heart is placed in another person's chest, the recipient's understanding of love might be enhanced by the memories generated from the donor.

One of my favorite patients, Boo Whitmer, shared with me her experience as a heart transplant recipient. Soon after her transplant surgery in 1999, she began experiencing a totally different feeling of love than she had before her surgery. When I asked if perhaps the difference in perception might be attributable to her gratitude for the lifesaving transplant, she assured me she did not think so because, as a cancer survivor years before, she had already embraced a profound gratitude for life.

Boo described her newly found way of loving as being able to experience love to a much deeper degree, at a much more spiritual level. This new experience of love offered her a much more complete appreciation of life. More importantly, it provided her a better understanding of death because she now had the living heart of a deceased person beating in her chest. She quipped: "I am so fortunate now because I have the capacity to love doubly!"

What she was describing was *metanoia*, Greek for a "change of heart." She experienced transformation in its purest sense. Her original heart's imprint of love had merged with the love contributed by another who had donated a heart to Boo.

We don't need to go to the extreme of having a heart transplanted in our chest in order to experience such an amalgamation of love! It happens with each tender touching of souls.

As it should be, each of us is different. One unique perspective on life and love comes from don Miguel Ruiz, MD, *New York Times* best-selling author of *The Four Agreements*.

In the early 1970s, don Miguel was involved in a near-fatal automobile accident. Hovering above his mangled body, he realized what needed healing were not only the fractured parts of his physical body and brain but his mind as well. Recovering, he purposefully redirected his energy back onto the ancestral path of transformational Toltec wisdom his predecessors had introduced to him years before.

In February of 2002, don Miguel suffered a massive heart attack that left him with barely enough heart function to sustain life. Over the course of the next several years, he developed significant congestive heart failure and because the flow of blood to all of his organs and muscles was so diminished, he endured incessant pain and suffered multiple organ-system failure. Throughout his ordeal, as excruciating as it was, don Miguel learned to accept the unrelenting pain as part of himself. He also learned the Second Agreement: "Don't take anything personally." He did not blame his disease or anyone else for his circumstance. As such, he felt no bitterness but instead experienced enlightenment.

Enduring eight years of agony, he ultimately underwent successful heart transplantation in October 2010, receiving the heart of a 20-year-old. Immediately after the lifesaving operation, the horrific pain he had lived with all those years disappeared.

The fortitude of this wise sage serves as a template for the rest of us on how to live life well, even when painful obstacles presented to us seem overwhelming. His zest for life, coupled with deep gratitude, has sprouted and flourished from the seed of ancient Toltec wisdom he had long ago forgotten.

"I am programmed to live, to survive," don Miguel shares. "After my heart attack, I said to my family, 'I'm not going to go home and wait for death to find me. Instead, I will look for death and enjoy my life the best I can,' I'm not afraid of death. I know I am immortal!"[39]

What keeps don Miguel Ruiz going is simple. It's love. "I keep loving wherever I go," he offers. "We were born to love. We don't need love. Whether people love me or not is secondary. I don't need their love, I *AM* love! What makes me happy isn't that someone loves me. What makes me happy is the love that comes out of me."

Don Miguel encourages us to: "…let everything we do and say be an expression of the beauty in our heart, always based on love."[40]

In his book entitled *The Afterlife Experiments*, Gary Schwartz, PhD, describes research involving two individuals, each being monitored with a brainwave test (EEG) and an electrocardiogram (EKG). The premise of the experiment was to determine if the cardiac electrical impulses from one subject could be sensed in the brain of another.

Schwartz explains that each and every cell in our body is bathed with electromagnetic "info-energy" from the heart. Through the process, every cell becomes enlightened to the nature of one's own unique heart, whose vital information is constantly being circulated.

Schwartz demonstrated that at the very least, this "info-energy" could reach and interact with the brain of someone in close proximity. Utilizing ultra-sensitive technology, he was able to document the presence of a circulating energetic memory created by this interaction and confirmed that EKG waves from one person's heart were detected in the second subject's brain. This very exciting discovery confirmed the interconnectivity between individuals, an implication of enormous significance.[41]

In further exploration of the concept of an electrical connection between people, Dr. Schwartz and Linda Russek, PhD, discovered that the sharing of this heart-brain information and energy between individuals just might explain the conveyance of love from one individual to another. In other words, a person can literally touch the heart of another.[42]

Each of us has spent countless hours with loved ones, being bathed in their loving cardiac "info-energy." Be it from the close proximity of your significant other sleeping in the bed beside you or the many hours you spent as a fetus in your mother's womb being lulled by her heartbeat, over time you accrue a memory of this information, the heart's individualized love signature.

This becomes a permanent part of the energy resonating within and from us. This memory, the spirit of love, outlasts the physical body, offering us immortality in that it can ultimately be passed on to our descendants long after we make our transition.

With love as its glue, such a connection can be tapped into at any time, bringing into closer proximity the memory of that love in much the same way that my father, who had "moved away," was able to remain inextricably connected to us. Such an association can be linked between loving souls who happen to be incarnated at the same point in time or, just as easily, it can form between those who lived thousands of years apart! Or as Rumi once shared:

"Love is from the infinite, and will remain until eternity. The seeker of love escapes the chains of birth and death."

EYES HAVE ALWAYS INTRIGUED ME. The glance of the eye is perhaps the most expressive form of communication we have; it conveys an innocent truthfulness.

It has been said the eyes are the portals to the soul. I became more cognizant of that profound observation years ago when my son, Tyler, brought the significance of a gaze to my attention.

One morning he and I went to the home of a man who was selling an antique oak bar. The seller was very pleasant and had a warm smile.

We spent about an hour conversing with the guy about the history of the bar, and as we were walking back to our truck, my four-year-old son shared with me his observation of the man we had just met. His description blew me away when he said, "Ya know, Dad, I *really* liked that man. He smiled with his eyes."

How perceptive! Tyler had spotted something I had totally missed. Yes, I had noticed the gentleman's kind demeanor, but Tyler had detected something on a much deeper level than I had. I was the recipient of a valuable lesson taught to me by my son, who was wise beyond his years. It was through Tyler that I became exquisitely aware of what the eyes are capable of conveying.

Several months later, a 42-year-old man presented to the ER in the midst of a massive heart attack. Being the invasive cardiologist on call, I was paged immediately to the emergency room. During my initial face-to-face conversation with the man, his eyes suddenly lost their focus as he went into cardiac arrest right before my eyes.

One cannot imagine a more profound experience than knowing of literally millions of images a person sees during his lifetime, you are the last one he sees before his death.

Fortunately, I was able to shock his heart back into rhythm with a defibrillator, resuscitating him back to life. His situation though, remained quite tenuous as his life was in significant jeopardy. I suggested to him that we immediately proceed to the cardiac cath lab to perform an emergent heart catheterization on him. I explained it was imperative that we attempt as soon as possible to open what I knew to be his totally blocked major coronary artery—one we commonly refer to as the "widow-maker".

To my dismay, he absolutely refused to proceed with any procedures until his wife arrived. As hard as I tried to convince him otherwise, he was resolute in his decision.

Upon her ultimate arrival over two hours later, I rushed back to his room in the coronary care unit. With his wife now at his bedside, I began my urgent plea for them to allow me to proceed with the emergent procedure as he was in the midst of a major heart attack. I explained in quite explicit terms that with or without the emergent procedure, he could very well die—in fact, he had already done so once today!

No sooner had those words left my lips than I felt the presence of someone else in the room. As I turned toward the corner of the room, I saw his daughter seated on a footstool. She appeared to be about the same age as my nine-year-old daughter, Laila. When our eyes met, I could see absolute fear in her innocent eyes, fear at least in part, exacerbated by my insensitivity.

With her eyes welling up with tears, her gaze halted me in my tracks. Kneeling down in front of her, tears began welling up in my eyes as well.

In life or death circumstances such as this, being able to maintain objectivity and focus are critical in being able to make split-second decisions that will likely impact the outcome. But at this moment, when I peered into this child's frightened eyes, I paused to refocus on what it was *she* was experiencing. I pictured myself as the patient and thought that if I were in that bed, I would hope my physician would have the compassion and sensitivity to take a moment to offer an explanation to my daughter at her level in order to allay what was likely the most terrifying experience of her young life.

In measured words, I carefully described her father's condition and offered reassurance to this young child that her daddy would, indeed, be okay. As I softly spoke to her, I could see relief slowly enter her eyes as a single tear slowly trickled down her left cheek. Dabbing it, I dried her tear and gave her a loving embrace as if she were my own.

In my line of work, there is an expression: "time is muscle." In the setting of a heart attack, the sooner an occluded artery can be re-opened, the more heart muscle can be preserved. Who knows what the outcome might have been had I been able to convince my patient to proceed with the catheterization before he had the chance to see his family and affirm his love?

What I do know is the energy in that room changed, guided by the gaze of a beautiful soul. What stayed with my patient was a stent to keep his artery opened. What stayed with me was the memory of an innocent child's hopeful gaze, peering deeply into my eyes, imploring me to keep her daddy safe.

WHEN OUR PHYSICAL BODY SPROUTS INTO BEING, two travel companions join the rapidly developing manifestation of a unique life form. This newly combined triumvirate watches together as miraculously, an exponential expansion of cells begins to unfold.

But with all the fanfare, many of us will fail to acknowledge the two fellow travelers that have joined our body. Despite the oversight, the triad will remain inextricably connected every single moment of every single day, traveling with one another on their conjoined journey. One of the compadres joining the physical incarnation is *Death,* the other ... is the *Soul.*

Many of us assume death waits to present itself until the time of our ultimate departure from life draws near. To the contrary, *Death* is there from the outset. In some form or another, it accompanies our passage from the healthy and vital days of our youth through the inescapable deterioration brought on by aging and disease.

All too often, we foolishly suppress the inevitability of death. And then one day, perhaps when we least expect it, life circumstances shock us into an enhanced awareness of death. Because we have ignored this companion for too long, when death starts knocking louder and louder at the threshold, we find ourselves too petrified to open the door. How we process the fear of what the Grim Reaper might have in store for us, determines how much of a paralyzing advantage he will be able to exert over us.

The most effective antidote for such distress is to deprive death of its foreignness. By recognizing and embracing this fellow traveler early in life, we can learn to simply get used to death over the course of time.

Becoming familiar with death doesn't have to be morbid. If encountered early enough, such cognizance can be immensely helpful in guiding us to accept the inevitability of our own demise without fear or trepidation.

Getting to know death doesn't have to be delayed until we are lying on our deathbed. To the contrary, it's much more fruitful to get to know one another while we're still in a state of wellbeing.

Death awareness can become a catalyst for change in one's life. It can occur at any time. Ebenezer Scrooge in Charles Dickens' *A Christmas Carol* undergoes a life-altering transformation after being visited by The Ghost of Christmas Yet to Come. Trembling, he watches the worldly possessions he worshipped in life being picked over like vegetables at a market. The epiphany comes as he visits his unkempt grave, realizing the loneliness he is now experiencing is the result of his sordid past.

He resolves to make a change. His conscious choice is to bid farewell to the selfish, mean-spirited life he has lived up to that point. In its place, a renewed outlook on life emerges as Ebenezer Scrooge discovers that it is not too late for him to get to know *Death*.

Contrary to common practice, children should not be shielded from death. Instead, they should be introduced to the true nature of life and its partner, *Death*. The earlier in life this groundwork is initiated, the more beneficial it becomes. It is far better to include children in the dying process despite the fact that sadness will likely accompany such involvement.

As much as we would like to protect our children from being exposed to death, it is a disservice to them when we do so. As such, we should gently introduce to them what they likely have already contemplated.

If we exclude children from a healthy grieving process, they are likely to be left feeling unprotected and vulnerable as they attempt to navigate such difficult terrain alone. This only magnifies their fear of abandonment and loneliness.

The mother of one of my best friends growing up was diagnosed with terminal cancer. Everyone knew she was going to die, a fear my eight-year-old friend also shared. Even though that critical piece of information was never shared with her directly, she knew.

I recall one evening our parents were going out for dinner together. It would be the last time the four of them would do so. As my father helped her frail mother into the car, my friend became hysterical. Crying uncontrollably, she was screaming, "I want my Mommy! Please don't leave me, Mommy! *PLEASEEEEE!!!*" she wailed, "Mommy, don't leave me!"

Watching her mother leaving in the car, my friend collapsed on the floor in front of a large picture window in our home. She never took her eyes off the darkened street and sobbed for over three hours, waiting for her mother to return. Every so often in her exhausted state of distress, she'd sigh, "I love you, Mommy. Please don't leave me."

As I recall the encounter, I can only imagine the overwhelming fear of abandonment my friend must have been feeling. No one had been up front with her about her mother's disease and impending death. For all she knew, her mother might not return from the dinner outing.

NONE OF US KNOW WHEN OR WHERE OUR PASSING WILL OCCUR, but rather than attempting to outrun death, we should learn as early in life as possible to anticipate this natural aspect of life without trepidation.

Just as the darkest of storm clouds have drought hidden within them, life has death concealed within it as well. Dying is not the end of life—it's quite the opposite. What we often refer to as death allows for the continuation of life that will remain forever manifested in the form of spirit. Our death becomes the fuel for the eternal journey of our third bedfellow, our *Soul*.

> *"To practice death is to practice freedom. A man who has learned how to die has unlearned how to be a slave."*
> ~ Michel de Montaigne, French essayist[43]

While death is considered by many to be the fiercest wound that can be inflicted on us, it is from such a mortal injury that the *Soul* appreciates that its spiritual expansion, its reason for being here, couldn't have come to fruition any other way. The vehicle to the soul's reunion with God is through that very death.

And when our time comes, the body and *Death*, two of the companions that have been our travel partners since birth will fall by the wayside, allowing the only immortal aspect of our being, our *Soul*, to continue on its portage back home unencumbered, carrying with it all of the knowledge and enlightenment accrued during this particular incarnation.

WHISPERS OF THE HEART:

1. Embrace the fact that *Death* accompanies our passage from birth through the relentless process of aging. Become familiar with your companion long before you'll need its services.

2. Death is a natural corollary of life. Every family member, regardless of his or her age, should be included in the experience. Becoming familiar with death doesn't have to be frightening. The more we try to protect our children from death, the greater a disservice it becomes to them. Better to gently expose them to what they have already contemplated. Our children will be stronger for the encounter. The experience, sad as it may be for them, can become fodder for growth.

3. Just as the darkest of storm clouds have drought hidden within them, life has death concealed within it as well. Dying is not the end of life—it's quite the opposite. So-called death is the continuation of life that will be manifest in the form of *Soul*.

CHAPTER 11

CONTINUATION

The seed dies into a new life, and so does man.
~ George McDonald

Last spring, I was tooling around rural Ohio and found myself at a bird swap meet. This was my first experience at a menagerie such as this. There were hundreds of birds! Every color, shape, and size was represented at this annual sale held in Amish country.

I came upon four baby black swans, cygnets as they are called, little puffballs of soft downy grayish-blue feathers. I picked up one. As he nestled into the comfort of my cupped hands, his beak, which had a trace of red coursing through its mostly steel-gray color, began stroking me.

Impulsively, I bought all four cygnets. Placing them carefully in a box, I began walking to my truck when it suddenly occurred to me that there was no mommy swan to take care of these babies. Who was going to nurture them? Who would show them how to grow up to be big swans?

As I looked down at them in their box, each of them looked back up at me, chirping almost as if to ask: "You'll take care of me, won't you?"

Little did I appreciate the bond that had just formed. It felt like what happens when you're dating someone, and she falls in love with you before you realize you have fallen in love with her. The cygnets and I had fallen for one another.

When I arrived home with my new fluffy family, I created a cozy space for them in our garage. They were too young and vulnerable to be left outside on their own.

Every morning I would carry each of them out, one at a time, to a fenced garden area where the four musketeers would huddle. Their ritual became a constant burrowing of themselves into the pile of each other. There was obvious contentment on their part as they clustered tightly with one another, sharing their collective warmth.

Every 20 minutes or so, I'd check on them; the two largest cygnets tended to knock over or sit on the smaller ones as they would dig into the mulch with their webbed feet.

On our third day together, I noticed only three of the cygnets in the garden. I ran over, looking for the runt of the litter, and found it upside down, its face completely buried under the mulch. Barely breathing, its body was completely flaccid. For a while, as I stroke its soft feathered back, it tried to lift its head, but all it could muster was enough energy to lift its head up only to have its neck and head plop to the other side. It was likely the cygnet had sustained irreversible brain damage due to oxygen deprivation.

Despite its poor prognosis, I continued to nurture it, gently caressing its body and talking to it, encouraging it to fight on. Using an eyedropper, I gave it trickles of water. But even with my efforts, its condition remained unchanged the remainder of the day.

That evening, I placed the other three cygnets back in their box. I put the incapacitated baby cygnet in a box by itself, hoping to protect it from further injury by its siblings.

When I awoke the next morning, the first thing I did was check on my babies, expecting to find my injured cygnet had succumbed during the night. To my delight, it was standing up and chirped at me as if to say: "Did you sleep in? Come on, buster. Let's get going! Where's breakfast? The day's a-wastin'!"

Over the next few months, I marveled as I chronicled the growth of my baby swans. Other than providing them food and shelter, I was a passive observer watching them as they discovered life and the variety of new experiences it had to offer.

There is an inexplicable innate knowledge imparted to creatures like my cygnets. How they knew to do certain things boggles the mind. Swans generally spend a lot of their time preening. They use their bills to fluff and rearrange their feathers while removing debris and insects lodged on them.

Swans cannot stay afloat in the water unless they first waterproof themselves. They have an oil gland at the base of their tail. Contorting their long necks, they reach back to their hind end, and using their bills to retrieve this oil, they spread it over their feathers. It becomes a continuous process for life.

What perplexes me is how these baby swans knew how to waterproof themselves. I certainly didn't teach them. Besides, I don't have that kind of flexibility!

As I lovingly cared for them, they reciprocated by sharing their love with me. Once they were mature enough to be set free on the water, I released them onto our lake. They found their new habitat invigorating. Whenever I would come outdoors, they would see me, and from across the lake, they'd start cooing in a way reserved only for me. They would come to me whenever I made a special sound.

Fall came and went as my babies continued to grow and expand their horizons. Winter arrived with a vengeance. The polar vortex deposited more snow and delivered more frigid temperatures than we had experienced in Ohio in more than two decades. Our 12-acre lake completely froze, which is something that rarely happens.

I wondered what the cygnets thought of the changing seasons. Their needs, of course, were met, but I tried to imagine the excitement and perhaps the fear they felt as winter settled in.

In similar fashion to a fish out of water, the frozen lake, unfortunately, put my babies at risk from coyotes that preyed on birds no longer able to escape by swimming away.

With temperatures dipping below zero and blustery gusts creating a wind chill factor of minus 20 degrees, my cygnets were also in danger of freezing to death. One morning, I took a bucket of feed to them across the lake. As I approached, I could see they were in imminent danger. Through the night, ice had accumulated on their feathers, literally encasing them. One cygnet had its eyes covered in ice and one nostril occluded by the icy shell. Their movements were dulled; no doubt they were suffering from hypothermia.

I coaxed them over to me and then, like Noah, I carried them two by two across the frozen lake, up the hill to our home, placing them in our heated garage. The trek across the lake was special in that I was able once again to hold my babies, cuddling them as I had when they fit in the palm of my hands. Only now they were almost full size.

Over the course of the next several days, the cygnets rebounded, improving as they regained lost weight, their strength returning. This precious time together in such close proximity allowed me to bond even more closely with them.

When the weather broke and temperatures rose to the mid-thirties, I released them once again back into the fluid part of the lake.

The following morning as the sun slowly began rising in the sky, darkness gradually being replaced with the early morning light, I looked out at the lake and saw four black spots on the still-frozen part of the lake. Each clump of bloodied black feathers stood out in stark contrast to the pristine white, snow-covered backdrop of the wintry tundra.

My babies' final resting spots were 30-40 feet apart from one another. The cygnets I had raised from infancy now lay motionless after what must have been a terrifying last few moments of life. Each had died alone, scattered from the place on the open bank where they had nested for the night, huddled together, conserving and sharing their heat, all the while being lulled into a false sense of security.

I ran down to the lake to confirm what I already knew had happened during the cover of night. My babies had been killed and partially devoured. I agonized over their seemingly senseless deaths, lamenting that I wasn't there to protect them. I felt angry at the heartless creature that had slaughtered my little ones who now, as unmoving as the frigid ice beneath them, lay lifeless on the frozen surface.

I don't recall ever being as close to a pet as I had grown to be with my cygnets. After all, I was their daddy. I was the one who had nurtured them through most of their lives. I was devastated as I walked back up to the house and into my office where, in my solitude with tears freely flowing down my cheeks, I grieved.

Two months later, with winter's icy grip still upon us, four dark frozen heaps remained on the surface of our ice-covered lake. Their carcasses tormented me every day. But as I hesitantly looked out the window on this particular morning, something changed in the way I processed the image of their remains. On this day, I felt persuaded by a higher energy to change my thought, to make a shift in my consciousness, to look at my perceived loss in a different light.

I came to acknowledge that the supreme sacrifice made by my cygnets had been purposeful. Their deaths had offered sustenance to another living creature whose right to survive was just as destined as that of my baby swans. I trusted the hunter in its own way had been respectful of the hunted it had consumed.

I meditated for a very long time that wintry morning as yet another layer of enlightenment unfolded for me. I thanked my cygnets for their sacrifice and for their contribution to the continuation of life. I held no ill will for the coyote that at some point in its lifetime would offer up its own sacrifice in the never-ending cycle of life. I knew that someday, I would do the same.

HE HAD LIVED A LONG AND ILLUSTRIOUS LIFE. My Uncle Jerry Lippman really wasn't a blood relative, but he sure seemed like it to me. I had the privilege of not only being his friend, but I also was able to serve as his cardiologist. He was the founder of GoJo Industries, the inventor of Purell. Even before the Covid-19 pandemic he had quite literally touched the lives of hundreds of millions across the globe!

Despite the miracles of modern medicine, we will all eventually transition. Uncle Jerry certainly did not possess immunity to the inevitability of life in that ultimately he succumbed to the ravages of congestive heart failure.

A week before he transitioned, his care was complemented with hospice. With their help, his last days were made comfortable. As he continued his step-by-step journey toward the next phase of life, he and his family were granted the gift of time to express their love, to say the necessary good-byes, and to begin the grieving process of mourning their looming loss. It was a special time of reflection for us all.

Uncle Jerry had reached the point in his journey where deep slumber had taken over. Peace enveloped him as his eyes, in rare moments of lucidity, focused on visions far away. His breathing became slower and more deliberate.

His nephew and my dear friend, Joe Kanfer, stood at the head of the bed. Several others were seated well away from the immediate vicinity of what was soon to become Uncle Jerry's deathbed.

His grandniece, Marcella, was seated next to Uncle Jerry. In her left arm, she cradled her newborn son.

What happened next was a beautiful scene that unfolded to me in a slow motion of magnificence. Even as Uncle Jerry's breathing became ever more shallow, it seemed to assume a deeper quality. At one point, he took in a deep breath. As he slowly exhaled, Joe reached down and placed his hand gently on Uncle Jerry's head. At the same moment, Marcella reached for Uncle Jerry's hand with her right hand, tenderly caressing it while holding her infant son in her other arm, breast-feeding him.

At that precise moment, I sensed Uncle Jerry's *ruach*, Hebrew for breath and spirit, as it was transferred through his breath, traveling to his nephew, then on to the next generation, his grandniece, and reaching his infant great-grandnephew.

The connection was marvelously powerful. Looking at the tiny hands of Uncle Jerry's great-grandnephew, I was reminded of a beautiful observation by Thich Nhat Hanh:

> *"If you look deeply into the palm of your hand, you will see*
> *your parents and all generations of your ancestors. All of*

them are alive at this moment. Each is present in your body.
You are the continuation of each of these people."[44]

I have come to understand this vessel I call my body is not mine. It's the vibrant continuation of my ancestors who still exist in some form within me. The unique DNA template I received from the genetic pools of my parents carries with it the entirety of the chromosomal history of all of those who have preceded me in life.

As an equal-opportunity recipient, it is incumbent upon me to accept each contribution of DNA that has been given me, whether perceived as good or bad. I must be receptive, opening my heart to each offering, just as those descendants of mine who have yet to be born will do with the genetic information I will ultimately pass on to them.

My descendants will carry not only my DNA but also that of my ancestors. The cells that comprise them will carry as their legacy my legacy and that of my great-grandfather and others. I am their continuation, their seed. Carrying even small increments of a predecessor into the future ensures each donor's immortality.

Because DNA replicates and is transferred to the next generation, there is no death.

"We should so live and labor in our time that what came to us
as a seed may go to the next generation as a blossom."
~ Henry Ward Beecher[45]

When a cloud transforms itself into rain, is it gone forever? If we are no longer attached to the appearance of the cloud, looking deeply into the rain, we can readily see that the cloud is still there.

Much like the perceived disconnection from departed loved ones, they aren't dead and gone forever just because we can no longer see or touch them. In order to maintain the connectivity, we must follow the energy of our loved ones. Uncle Jerry's last breath of air carried with it vapors from his lungs that coalesced with other molecules of moisture. Eventually they joined other droplets of water, becoming a rain cloud that released its moisture to the earth, nurturing countless beautiful wildflowers.

Accepting the continuation of life, and not its death, helps us let go of the fear of dying.

MY FAVORITE TIME OF DAY is the moment just before daylight inches its way onto the early morning landscape. You can actually feel life coming to life.

One special moment occurred for me several months back. I stepped outside, marveling at a new day being born. Sitting in the darkness, I began my morning meditation. All was silent. Everything remained asleep and tranquil.

Soon, the first light of this fresh new day began to emerge, awakening all from their silent slumber. Slowly, the stillness began to percolate with life. As the darkness became light, nature began vibrating marvelous energy. As I took in a deep cleansing breath, I acknowledged another day had hatched on this third rock from the sun. Even though its cycle was predictable, the new day unfolding would be unique, just as all of the trillions of days preceding this particular glorious morning had been.

With the trumpeted call from the lead bird, all of the geese that had spent the night on our lake took to flight. The flock rose higher and higher, piercing the early morning mist, and their arduous effort seemed to ease the further aloft they became.

As if awakened by a bugle call, many other birds initiated their morning revelry, professing their gratitude for the warmth of the sun.

This is the flow of life, the energy of the Universe. If we allow, this energy can vibrate within us, providing our spirit with rejuvenating renewal.

My day had begun with an all-encompassing gratitude for the wonders just observed. The cycle continued for me until the veil of evening descended. Then, everything began to slow down until silence once again intervened.

Even though life is impermanent, the ripples our lives create continue beyond what we consider the so-called end of our lives.

Each contribution we make to the Universe is like a pebble thrown into a still pond, creating a ripple that continues in an ever-widening circle. Despite the impermanent nature of our physical lives, our energy continues forever. It is not essential that our identity, our acts, and even our memories survive. The important thing is that our ripples continue, enhancing everything touched by them.

WHISPERS OF THE HEART:

1. Acknowledge the supreme sacrifice all of the many animals and plants have made to ensure your sustenance. As you consume their energy, which now becomes yours, be grateful. At some point, each of us will be called upon to donate ourselves to the circle of life. It should be our privilege to do so. Offer yourself back to nature. Become part of the building blocks of life that are yet to come.

2. Follow the flow of life, the energy of the Universe that provides our spirit with rejuvenation.

3. DNA replicates and is transferred to the next generation. Because of this continuation, there is no death.

CHAPTER 12

WHAT DREAMS MAY COME

*That which lies beyond our fondest imagination of the
dreams, aspirations, and goals in this life will fall far
short of what we will experience in the next!*
~ Art Blair

W hat is real?
  Most would agree that when we interact with the physical world, our perception of this material space represents reality.

But what happens when, in the midst of deep slumber, we find ourselves in a dream state? While there, doesn't that experience appear to be as animated and equally as authentic as the physical world?

Now, contemplate arriving in heaven. A major shift in perception will likely occur upon entering such a sanctified space, with heaven's bliss becoming as real to us as the physical and dream worlds we left behind. From such a sacred celestial perch, we become passive observers, watching as our physical self tumbles back to Earth like an expendable launch rocket being discarded in space. In contrast, our soul gains the necessary altitude and momentum in order to maintain its new trajectory in the afterlife.

Which of these experiences—the material realm, the dream state, or the afterlife—are in fact real? Is it possible all three can be?

Where did the notion of an afterlife originate? All of the world's major religions affirm that some form of existence continues once the physical body dies.

Ancient hieroglyphics suggest that, at the very least, prehistoric man was aware of some power greater than himself. The ancient Egyptian was promised a fulfilling life in the hereafter. In preparation for the afterlife, his burial tomb was furnished with a wide variety of utensils, clothing, and nutriments that would make eternity an easier existence for him.

So, the question becomes: *is there life after death?* If so, what will it look like? Might it mirror what male Muslims anticipate, where they will be provided all the pleasures imaginable from 72 full-bosomed virgins? Or will the afterlife offered be similar to what the Native American anticipates finding, a happy hunting ground replete with all the bison one could ever need?

The logical, scientific part of my mind tells me if there is an afterlife, then there will be only two ways to unequivocally confirm its existence. One must die and come back to share the near-death experience with the rest of us, or we must be fortunate enough to catch a glimpse of the next world, perhaps through an after-death communication (ADC).

Bill and Judy Guggenheim, authors of *Hello From Heaven*, compiled extensive data on more than 3,500 firsthand accounts of ADCs. According to them, ADCs provide evidence for life after death, confirming that the energy of life and the love we share with one another are eternal.

An ADC is a spiritual experience that occurs when a person is contacted directly by another who has already departed this life. It doesn't require mediums or psychics, nor are any rituals necessary to make the connection.

According to the Guggenheims, an ADC is a communication initiated by the deceased, the purpose of which is to offer hope and reassure loved ones left behind that the departed are indeed still connected. They also want their living loved ones to be assured that when the time comes for them to cross, those in the hereafter will be there to assist them in the transition.

ADCs are universal. They have been described over the centuries. They cross all religious boundaries and are revealed to a socio-economically, educationally, racially, and occupationally diverse group of people ranging in age from the very young to the old.

Perhaps the most famous ADC occurred in Christianity. The return of Jesus from the dead laid the foundation upon which Christian doctrine rests. According to the New Testament, after his execution by Roman crucifixion, Jesus was buried. Three days later, his followers discovered his tomb to be empty. It was believed that he was resurrected. The purpose of Jesus' return was to demonstrate the power God had over death, proof that life was indeed eternal.

Sadly, many mental health professionals and some clergy dismiss reported ADCs as not being credible, ascribing them to hallucinations, delusional states, or even to lucidity being numbed by pain and antianxiety medications.

The Guggenheims describe a number of different forms of ADCs. Some of which include:

1. *Sentient ADCs* are one of the most common types. It occurs when an individual develops an intuitive sense that he or she is in the presence of a deceased loved one.
2. *Auditory ADCs* involve hearing a voice. Most describe it as hearing a voice inside of their head with the knowledge that it originated outside of their mind.
3. In *Tactile ADCs*, which occur less commonly, the description is of feeling a touch, an embrace—a more intimate kind of ADC.
4. An *Olfactory ADC* involves the smelling of a fragrance, an aroma that carries the potential to induce a strong emotional response.
5. *Visual ADCs* generally occur as either partial or full appearances. One might only be able to see part of the body, a face, or if the whole body appears, it might be seen as less than solid and more translucent.[46]

Often at death, the veil between the material world and the spirit world becomes very thin. This purportedly allows to be seen the inhabitants of the eternal world who have come to take the departed home.

DURING RELIGIOUS UPBRINGING, MANY HAVE BEEN TAUGHT WHAT HEAVEN IS LIKE. Some of us believe that we will be greeted at the Pearly Gates by an anthropomorphic figure who resembles an old man with a long white beard, wearing a flowing diaphanous white robe, sitting on his throne. To others, heaven is quite different.

When my daughters were five, four, and two years old, our family attended a dinner during the High Holy Days of Judaism at the home of very close friends, Mimi and Stewart Surloff. The group numbered in the twenties. The adults were seated at a large dining room table and the children at small card tables placed throughout the living room area. Mimi's father was seated at the head of the table. I was on his immediate left. In the middle of a joke he was telling about a doctor and a lawyer, he suddenly slumped over. At first, we all thought it was part of the joke because he was the consummate storyteller and typically very dramatic in his presentations.

It soon became clear that this was no laughing matter. He was in a full cardiac arrest. I immediately began performing CPR as someone else called 911. Once the paramedics arrived, we worked feverishly for 15 or 20 minutes attempting to resuscitate him. Ultimately, he was transported to the emergency room of the hospital where I practiced. I accompanied him in the ambulance, continuing CPR the entire trip. Sadly, despite the heroic efforts of many, he did not survive.

Upon returning to our friends' home, everyone was in shock at what had been collectively experienced. The immediate concern of those of us with young children was the emotional trauma this experience might have on them.

I recall my two-year-old daughter, Britt, walking around the dining room, calling out, "Where'd that sick boy go? Where'd that sick boy go?"

Quite emotional, my wife, Angela, and I gathered our children around us. When Angela explained to them that Mimi's father had passed away, our five-year-old daughter, Mattie-Rose, asked, "Daddy, where is he now?"

I remember struggling to answer her question in a way she might comprehend. I described heaven in terms I had been taught as a child. I shared with my kids that heaven was a beautiful place where there is no pain or suffering. I described to them that heaven is very peaceful; it is where God sits on a golden throne, surrounded by many wise elders and all of our previously departed loved ones.

Once I finished my explanation, I remember feeling somewhat comforted by her response when Mattie-Rose sweetly said, "Hmm, Daddy, heaven sounds like a nice place to be."

While my description had satisfied her curiosity and put this tragic event into a neat little package for her, I felt sad and hypocritical because what I had described to my children was not at all what I believed to be the truth. At the time, I didn't know where dead people went. My lack of conviction, however, awakened within me a desire to begin the journey of searching for that truth, an exploration that continues to this day. I believe this quest for enlightenment is one of the main reasons I am currently writing this book and why it has decided to write me.

Maybe there is the heaven I described to my children, a place that lies somewhere over the rainbow beyond the majestic swirl of the galaxies. Or as an old Eskimo proverb suggests:

> *"Perhaps they are not stars, but rather openings in heaven*
> *where the love of our lost ones pours through and shines*
> *down upon us to let us know they are happy."*

Regardless of what form it takes or where it lies, experiencing heaven, bliss, or Nirvana will likely be the ultimate experience in the attainment of higher consciousness.

WHISPERS OF THE HEART:

1. ADCs have been described for centuries. They cross all religious boundaries and for many, provide evidence for life after death. ADCs suggest that the energy of life and the love we share with one another are eternal.

2. What does heaven look like? Is it what you were taught in religious school, or have your thoughts about it changed? Heaven may be nothing more than a reflection of your understanding or a product of your religious and cultural beliefs. Either way, your heaven will be just that...your heaven.

3. Be receptive to the messages from beyond. From *My Favorite Martian*, a television sitcom in the early 1960s, the marooned space traveler who had landed on Earth could only communicate with those back on Mars when his antenna was activated, rising from the crown of his head. In similar fashion, in order to catch a glimpse of the next world through an after-death communication, your figurative antennae must be actuated. Your receptivity to the messages being offered must be fine-tuned. Only then will you be able to hear the silent message of those having transitioned before you.

PART IV:

THE DEATH OF DEATH

CHAPTER 13

GOOD GRIEF

Grief and its unique healing powers take us from
meaninglessness to meaningfulness again.
~ David Kessler

The mourning process is a personal one. Each of us navigates such an experience in our own unique way. Because you're not walking in another person's moccasins, you can't be judgmental of the way he chooses to grieve. It is impossible to grasp the paralyzing pain and loneliness he likely feels. No one can see with clarity what he sees because his or her vantage point is a completely different one.

Many of us, especially those heralding from earlier generations, have been conditioned to remain strong in the face of tragedy. For a man, shedding tears used to be considered a sign of weakness. In fact, Senator Ed Muskie, the front-runner in the 1972 presidential election, lost his bid shortly after crying on camera after an article was circulated attacking his wife.

Grieving is generally more difficult for men than it is for women. For males, not giving ourselves permission to grieve can cause a damming-up of painful emotions that prevent the natural flow of feelings required to make it through the sorrow.

The process of mourning can last a very long time, especially if the loss is an unexpected one. Sudden death is one of the most difficult experiences to digest. In an instant, everything dramatically changes. Our world is suddenly upended as we descend in a free fall of unimaginable proportions.

There has been no warning or preparation and to make matters worse, we may have been deprived of the chance to say good-bye.

Bereavement is not static; it's an ever-changing, moving target. It may depart only to resurface at a later date in a different form, precipitated by a totally different inciting event. The fact that grief comes and goes tells us that we have yet to fully resolve all of grief's associated issues.

Dr. Elisabeth Kübler-Ross, in her groundbreaking text *On Death and Dying*, describes five stages of grief that the dying, as well as those remaining behind, generally experience. They include denial, anger, bargaining, depression, and acceptance.[47]

Not everyone goes through each of these five stages, nor do we necessarily experience them in linear fashion. We can vacillate from one stage to another only to find ourselves back in an earlier one.

Stage One, DENIAL, generally appears as disbelief that I am going to die. A common response is: "Obviously, the hospital must have made a mistake and confused my test results with those of someone else." The shock experienced in the denial stage may occur because it's just too early for us to process the trauma of the impending loss in any other way.

There is no set amount of time we remain at this or any of the five stages. Once denial begins to fade, the reality of the situation begins to slowly surface.

Stage Two, ANGER, generally surfaces once denial has run its course. This stage can appear in the form of anger directed at God, at the family, at the doctors or nursing staff, or even at the person who has died or is dying!

Anger can take many forms. It's a normal emotion, despite the fact that we might feel guilty expressing it. It's a necessary phase that must be worked through in order for healing to occur. It can be a useful tool through which our underlying emotions can begin to percolate to the surface where they can be acknowledged and expressed in healthy ways.

Recently I spoke with a mother whose daughter had been gravely injured in a car accident. She had sustained a significant traumatic brain injury. This mother was very disappointed and quite angry that her friends and her daughter's acquaintances had stopped coming around.

Having experienced a similar response from our son's friends and families, I would imagine that her daughter's associates felt profound sadness at seeing this young, previously vibrant girl in such a state. All too often, the response to situations that are difficult is ... avoidance.

At first, my suggestion to the mother was to try and understand how uncomfortable her friends and those of her daughter must feel. Then I realized that this mother's anger was serving a distinct purpose for her. As destructive as it appeared to others, her anger became a vehicle that provided for her a bridge to healing.

I have personally experienced such healing arising from anger. It was during my father's infirmity due to prostate cancer, I became enraged that a good God could do this to such a kind soul. I remember one day in particular. Dad had been quite ill and was hospitalized. Mom was running on empty. She'd sit at Dad's side 23 hours a day, leaving only long enough to drive home to take a quick bath and change clothes. She was an emotional and physical wreck.

I had planned a weekend away with some friends at the University of Kentucky. I had been looking very forward to getting away from the sadness, but when it came time to depart, I realized that my leaving at such a critical time for selfish reasons was the wrong thing to do. No one forced me to change my plans, but I just knew it wasn't right for me to leave Mom alone for the weekend.

The decision I made to stay didn't keep my erupting volcano of anger from being loosed. I remember throwing a handful of pens against the wall of my bedroom, splattering ink everywhere. As I was expressing anger in such a destructive manner, I was also observing myself doing so as I tried to understand the emotion.

As outsiders observing another person venting rage, we may encourage the individual to work through her anger stage as quickly as possible, judging such anger as being an inappropriate expression. But we must remember that it takes time to steer through the pain, and each of us must work through the anger phase at our own pace.

Stage Three, BARGAINING, is the phase in the process of grieving that involves attempts at negotiating away the immense pain being suffered. It is usually the briefest of the five stages and amounts to an attempt to postpone the inevitable.

Promises are offered up to a higher power that is believed to have control over the dreaded circumstance. In lamenting the trauma or death that has intervened in one's life, bartering with God, whether it seems rational or not, often takes the form of a vow that may set a self-imposed deadline. Such a pledge to God might be to allow me to live long enough to walk my daughter down the aisle at her wedding. Or it might be a promise that if my quadriplegic son is allowed to walk again, I will attend religious services every week for the rest of my life.

In desperate times, desperate actions need to be taken. We will barter with anyone we think can relieve our suffering. On occasion, a pact might even be made with the devil.

Stage Four, DEPRESSION, is a normal and natural emotion to experience, but all too often, our well-intentioned friends, family, and even our physicians try to push us through this phase too quickly.

Losing a loved one *is* depressing, and it's only natural that we feel that way when grieving the loss of someone dear to us.

Up to this point, while sadness has prevailed, the person has been able to muster enough energy to fight through the first three stages of denial, anger, and bargaining. In this, the fourth stage of grieving, there doesn't appear to be anything that can change the ultimate course of events. Generally, the grieving person has depleted energy stores to the point of no longer being able to fight the good fight.

Unfortunately, in our pharmaceutically driven society, we tend to medicate with antidepressants in order to help the grieving individual through the ordeal. In doing so, paradoxically, we mask and obscure the experience. Grievers are not mentally ill, we're just experiencing an appropriate response to something very sad.

There are a few who, in rare circumstances, get stuck in this phase. Their grief becomes pathological and might require intense counseling and the short-term use of pharmaceuticals. But generally with time, depression usually dissipates and departs once it has served its purpose.

Stage Five, ACCEPTANCE, the final stage, comes when we acknowledge and learn to live with the loss. It occurs when the conscious decision is made to begin embracing life once again. In doing so, we engage with the living, reaching out to them as we begin to move forward. For the terminally ill, this might include getting one's affairs in order. It might even involve helping loved ones come to grips with the inevitability of their impending crossing.

Peace begins to percolate into the milieu as the individual comes to accept whatever may come her way.

THROUGHOUT LIFE, MANY DOORS OPEN AND MANY, WITHOUT WARNING, SLAM SHUT ON US. When we are caught off guard, closings can feel extremely unfair. The door of life closing behind us feels like it is forever severing the connections with those we love.

The door might also become bolted shut on previous good physical health, causing us to lose a particular physical capability. Whether the result of an accident, disease, or the aging process, closing doors that will never reopen can cause pain and suffering, losses that can seem overwhelming.

As celebrated in the Jewish faith during the High Holy Day of Yom Kippur, Jews pray:

"Open for us the gate—at the hour of the closing of the gate."

What we can find if we are receptive is that as one door slams shut behind us, another one gently opens up ahead. Accept the closings. They are shutting in perfect order.

It is always better to openly acknowledge what you're facing, regardless of how difficult accepting it might be. The gaping wound of a looming death, whether it's your own or that of a loved one about to transition, needs attention paid to it in order to commence the healing process.

When a parent loses a child, that death screams out for an answer to the question, *Why? Why does such an injustice of nature have to happen to someone so young?*

As parents, we are supposed to die long before our children. Isn't that the natural order of things? On occasion, though, this orderly fashion somehow goes terribly awry. Such a premature demise alters our previous anticipation of how life should unfold.

Louis Acompora was a 14-year-old freshman at Northport High School in New York. He was a member of a beautiful family that shared a deep and abiding love for one another. He represented all of the amazing ideals that a parent desires of a child.

Louis was constantly striving to become a better person. He was a bright, energetic, and handsome young man with captivatingly beautiful blue eyes.

He was an athlete in superb physical condition and loved the game of lacrosse. Louis was excited to be playing in his first freshman lacrosse game. He was his team's co-captain and its starting goalie. He had been preparing for this moment for many years. His father, John, had been his coach, mentoring him in the sport he himself had enjoyed as a youngster.

It was March 25th, the year 2000. Life was about to change.

Both John and his wife, Karen, were at the game, proudly watching their son fulfill his dream of playing freshman lacrosse. It was a cool early spring afternoon, and life was good. The game was moving along. The jitters had left him and Louis was in a groove, playing very well.

At one point, he blocked a routine shot with his body, just the way he had been taught. Wearing the prescribed chest protector, sanctioned by the sport and his school, Louis was struck in the chest by a ball traveling close to 30 mph.

The impact caused Louis to stagger for a moment, and then he collapsed to the turf without even trying to break his fall. The effect of the ball striking his chest directly over his heart thrust Louis into ventricular fibrillation (VF), a chaotic heart rhythm disturbance. He had suffered commotio cordis, a life-threatening cardiac event. None of those present had ever heard of such a thing. Within a millisecond, rather than pumping efficiently, his heart was left quivering ineffectually. In that instant, his brain and other vital organs were now without oxygen or circulating blood.

At first, no one responded, assuming that he had just gotten knocked to the ground. When he didn't move, several teammates rushed to his side, soon followed by his coach and trainer.

Louis was unconscious but still breathing. The breaths were not normal respirations, however. The coach initially suggested that they not touch Louis, believing he had just gotten the wind knocked out of him. Louis was demonstrating what is referred to as agonal respirations, which is the body's last, futile attempt at breathing.

Karen implored her husband to go out onto the field to see what was wrong.

As John reached Louis' side, he knew his only son was in deep trouble. He had already begun turning blue from lack of adequate circulation. CPR was initiated, and 911 was called.

What no one there knew at the time was that for every minute Louis remained in a cardiac arrest, his chance of survival would drop by 10 percent. Nationwide, the average response time of paramedics is eight to twelve minutes. That is why of the 400,000 Americans who sustain a cardiac arrest every year, the overall survival rate is a dismal 3-5 percent if the only action taken is calling 911.

If 911 is called and CPR initiated, survival can double to 6-10 percent. But if 911 is notified, CPR is begun, and an early shock is delivered from an Automated External Defibrillator, or AED, the chances of survival can be well over 50 percent!

Unfortunately, it would be over 12 minutes before the emergency response team arrived to assist Louis. If you do the math, by the time they got there, Louis' chances of survival were zero.

The paramedics attempted to resuscitate Louis as best they could under the circumstances with multiple shocks to his heart using a defibrillator. Sadly, on the lacrosse field, in front of his teammates, in front of his friends, and in front of his parents, Louis Acompora experienced sudden cardiac death.

The travesty is that his death was potentially treatable. He had no structural heart disease, no congenital heart defect. His perfectly healthy heart had sustained blunt chest trauma that resulted in a heart rhythm disturbance that cost him his life. Had an AED been available, the young life of Louis Acompora would have likely been saved.

How does a parent handle such a tragic and sudden death? The Acomporas grieved. Their grief was at times overwhelming as the reality of the unfathomable began to settle in. They endured the five stages of grief described above by Dr. Kübler-Ross. But, somewhere within their profound heart-wrenching pain, a recurrent mantra began to slowly surface: Karen and John knew that Louis wouldn't want them to spend the rest of their lives sad. They knew he'd want them to turn their tragedy into something positive.

What began emerging for them was a shift in their thought, a change that enabled them to begin overcoming the unimaginable. They wondered how something positive could ever be generated from such a profoundly negative experience.

Karen and John's renewal of spirit came in the form of The Louis J. Acompora Memorial Foundation, which was established to raise awareness of sudden cardiac death (SCD) in kids. Their efforts to educate the public to better understand what causes children to die from cardiac arrest culminated in the passage of "Louis' Law" in the state of New York, legislation, which mandated that every public high school must have an AED. The foundation has also raised hundreds of thousands of dollars to purchase AEDs for schools.

Louis' purposeful mission continues to be manifest through the relentless efforts of his parents, resulting in the saving of over 100 lives thus far! And that number doesn't include all of the many hearts that have been forever touched as a result of the sacrifice made by Louis, one I believe he would happily make again.

How many of us go through a much longer lifetime without ever truly making a difference in the world. Louis, in his short 14 years, has touched and continues to touch thousands of lives.

> *"What we have done for ourselves alone dies with us; what we have done for others in the world remains and is immortal."*
> ~ *Albert Pike*[48]

Of course, the ultimate goal is being able to move through such profound grief, while discovering its meaning. But not everyone is able to discover such a purpose.

Grief can be a confusing process. At times, the paradoxical emotions may leave us conflicted. For a protracted illness, relief is perhaps an easier concept to accept. After a loved one has endured years of intense pain and misery, death can actually become a welcomed relief for the one transitioning, as well as for his family who has watched helplessly as an ocean of suffering has been endured.

To succeed in the process, we must be patient, taking the time necessary to allow good grief to germinate from the pain and suffering. In doing so, we will be led on to a peaceful path of acceptance and healing.

WHISPERS OF THE HEART:

1. Learn to be grateful for your suffering as gratitude opens the doors of opportunity, allowing you to work through the turmoil and achieve transformation of the heart.

2. Each of us grieves in our own unique way. The five stages of grief include denial, anger, bargaining, depression, and ultimately, acceptance. Every phase is experienced differently for each person. Not everyone goes through all five stages, nor is it necessary to experience them in linear fashion. In fact, you might vacillate from one to another and then find yourself back at an earlier stage you thought you had

already mastered. Remember, it simply takes time to navigate through such agony. Work through each stage of the process at your own speed. Don't allow others to dictate the pace for you.

3. Grief that remains unexpressed is likely a wound that will fester and never heal. Only when experienced in an open and honest fashion will grief diminish to the point of allowing you to return to living life as it was intended. Be gentle on yourself.

CHAPTER 14

THE PRIVILEGE OF PAIN

We must embrace pain and burn it as fuel for our journey.
~ Kenji Miyazawa

Will the dreadful pain ever go away, and should it? Life in its impermanence is destined to change. It always has been that way and always will be. The joy of finding the perfect mate, raising a beautiful and healthy family, crafting a successful career, and finding the home of our dreams is the endgame of many. But in an instant, all can be lost. Everything we dare to cherish undergoes the process of change. Lasting happiness can never be found until we are able to release the attachment to what once was. Until we learn to let go, we will remain trapped in the revolving door of pain and disappointment.

One of the most difficult aspects of suffering is the dread of being trapped in our perceived agony forever. Hopelessness invades like a cancer, metastasizing into the deepest crevasses of our souls. When we are buried within the loneliness of loss, it is nearly impossible to envision a way out of such interminable pain.

We feel disconnected from everyone and everything. Such loneliness will destroy us unless we can discover its purpose. Is there a reason for such suffering? Might there be a purpose for the pain? Great minds have pondered this question for ages.

Viktor Frankl found such purpose. While being held captive in Auschwitz, the infamous Nazi concentration camp, he scratched

Man's Search for Meaning with pencil on pieces of tattered paper. Persevering as millions were slaughtered, he observed paradoxically that the oldest and the most frail of inmates somehow survived while the strongest-appearing prisoners did not.

His understanding became clear when he realized that those who discovered a reason to live and who had set goals for themselves transcended to a place of higher consciousness. In doing so, they found meaning within such a horrific existence.

As Frankl encouraged: "Human life, under any circumstances, never ceases to have meaning, and that this infinite meaning of life includes suffering and dying, privation and death."[49] He came to fully understand his search for meaning through Friedrich Nietzsche's thoughts: "If you have a *why* to live for, you can bear with any *how*."

Everyone experiences suffering in some form or another. Rather than being isolated in our individual agony, our pain is meant to be shared. Suffering is a natural aspect of life. If we come to accept the lessons suffering has to offer and use the tutorial purposefully, painful encounters can become a fertile milieu for growth that propel us onto the next plateau of our transcendent path of enlightenment.

Through heightened awareness of our suffering, we begin accepting it as it is, without judgment. We come to discover suffering is not a punishment. To the contrary, it is a gift from God, available to us all as a tool from which to gain great wisdom.

For Buddhists, the Tonglen practice brings meaning to suffering by encouraging followers to transcend their own suffering while learning to appreciate the universality of pain. In doing so, they dedicate their suffering to those who suffer along with them.

A common theme is found in the story of the last few days in the life of Jesus. As he faced his own inevitable death, he asked God for strength, praying that through his death and the accompanying anguish he would likely endure, he would be able to dedicate his suffering to others, relieving them of their own misery.

What Jesus, Buddha, and others have taught us is that we must find a way to give back to life, even if it's in the form of our own suffering and death. How tragic it would be to experience the pain of dying, believing that it served no useful purpose. Better to share our suffering with the rest of the Universe, petitioning God to bless our suffering so that it might be purposeful to others.

It's only when we learn to accept the suffering and its universal nature that the pain becomes not only tolerable but potentially constructive.

Ally Willen was a 20-year-old college student from my hometown studying abroad in New Zealand. On a four-day hike with two of her roommates in Mt. Aspiring National Park, Ally was swept into a raging river and lost her young life.

Her sister, Emily, gained remarkable insight from the sadness and wrote *The Privilege of Pain*:

> People always say it gets easier. This is what they tell you when your mind is so clouded in despair and sorrow that the only way you can possibly cope with the grief is to go numb. Through the haze of dull numbness you can hear people gently assuring you, "It will get better in time," and "It won't always be this hard," and "There will be a day when you don't feel like this."
>
> All well-intentioned statements of course, and in the dazed stupor that follows the trauma and shock of losing someone you love, you find yourself clinging to such statements in much the same way a drowning man might cling to a buoy amidst a roaring sea.
>
> As time goes on, however, and the stupor begins to lift, the numbness begins to lessen as well. And then the pain fully sets in. It is a pain unlike anything that can be described, a pain so profound that it cannot be adequately captured by mere words in the English language.
>
> In the beginning, such debilitating pain devours every waking moment of your existence. There is scarcely a

reprieve from the heartbreak and when there is, it often feels jaded, unreal, not right. The pain becomes the cloak, which you wear everywhere you go.

At first you hate the pain. You try desperately to escape from it, try to free yourself from it in any conceivable way possible. You distract yourself and attempt to numb the raging storm inside of you with alcohol, drugs, sleep, food, travel, books, music, yoga—anything, simply *anything* you can get your hands on that might even remotely subdue the waves that threaten to exhaust you.

And when you cannot dull the pain through any of the above means, then you finally succumb to it, plunging into it headfirst. You scream and scream and scream, whether your cries are vocalized out loud or exist only inside of your own mind and heart.

Eventually, after what feels like an eternity you begin to realize that there is no escape. You realize that you can struggle against the pain all you want, but in the end, it is the equivalent of banging your head repeatedly against a brick wall.

Deep pain is the price of deep love, and once you start to understand the consequences of that love, something inside of you begins to shift. The pain starts to become a part of what you are. You carry it with you wherever you go and in all that you do. You carry it with you when you walk outside of your house; when you meet someone new for the first time; and when you see an old friend for the first time since "it" happened. You carry it with you when you go to sleep at night and often it is the first thing that greets you when you open your eyes the next morning. You carry it with you when you are alone and when you are with others, when you attend weddings and funerals and graduation parties.

But it starts to become less of a burden and more of a privilege to always carry the pain when you stop fighting it and begin to appreciate its reason for being there.

After some time passes you start to realize that you don't want the pain to go away, because the pain is the result of love. It is the tangible, visceral evidence of a life that was well-lived, of a relationship that was cherished, and of a deep and abiding love that is enduring throughout all time, surpassing even the transition we call death.

The pain is not the enemy unless we perceive it as so. It can be viewed as a heavy and heart-breaking cross to bear or we can choose to view it as an honor, because carrying the pain means that we were privileged enough to have had that beautiful person in our lives.

So often when a loved one passes the first thing people tell us is, 'I'm so sorry.' I heard this phrase many times after my sister first passed. Again, well-intentioned statements of course; but in my heart and mind I often thought to myself, I'm not sorry. No, I am not sorry about a life that was lived fully and to its highest potential; I am not sorry about a girl who was so passionate and brave about doing what she loved that she put everything on the line; and I am not sorry that I was fortunate enough to have had this miraculous human being as my sister for twenty precious years.

Instead of telling me you're sorry, I thought to myself, you should tell me congratulations. Congratulations, because you were lucky enough to have known such a special and beautiful person.

Where other people see tragedy, I choose to see triumph. Often this universe works in ways that are difficult for us humans to understand. If we can look closely enough, what appears on the surface as tragic might actually just be a completed life, a victory in and of itself.

People say twenty years is too short, and on the surface it certainly seems that way. But perhaps for my sister and for all those other souls who departed this earth at a young age, perhaps it was time enough. Twenty years was just enough for Ally to inspire a legacy, to change people's lives, and to help heal this world.

How we decide to view the pain will color our entire mindset. If we see the pain as the enemy and struggle against it, then we will also see a lot to be sorry about. We will see an unspeakable tragedy. If, however, we view the pain as a privilege, if we view it as an emblem of love, then we may just be able to glimpse the underlying ornate perfection and order that orchestrates all of the events in our lives.

My pain indeed does follow me everywhere I go. But it is no longer a terrifying monster that I need to escape from; it has shifted and morphed now into a comfortable traveling companion. I welcome him when he knocks and allow him to come in, with the full awareness that one day his visits will become less and less frequent. But will he ever go away completely? I think not, nor do I want him to. He is a necessary visitor, a welcome guest in my home. I honor his presence fully when he comes.

People who say it will get easier don't understand. It's not the pain that goes away. It doesn't get any easier, ever—the pain of missing my sister will be just as deep twenty years from now as it is today. What changes is your relationship to the pain. Your acceptance of the pain shifts and you become more familiar with it, until you get to the point where you accept its presence in your life, even welcome it, because you understand that the pain represents the strength of your love. And while the pain may always be there, the love will always be there too—that undying, constant, continuous, pure unconditional love.[50]

THROUGH THE GRACE OF GOD, I have been offered a wondrous gift—a transformative and different way to view experiences. I have discovered a new way to interpret adversity, a way to transform my suffering into insight.

It wasn't until our son, Tyler, sustained a life-altering spinal cord injury that I came to appreciate the vast potential for growth offered by such a so-called catastrophe. It was in the midst of experiencing excruciating agony of unimaginable magnitude that an awakening emerged in me.

I learned how not to reject the pain of such adversity, how not to deny or ignore the hurt. I learned instead to embrace it. What I came to realize was that by working through the turmoil, I was able to discover goodness within the hardship and more importantly, what lies beyond suffering.

Through this struggle, as I embraced the privilege of pain, I discovered an elevating appreciation of life. I came to know that hidden within the personal pain and turmoil of challenging sufferings, great wisdom lies. Such an understanding cannot be gleaned from a book; it's only through the living of life that such special insight can be learned. Only from experiencing pain ourselves can we learn how to first heal ourselves and then assist others to do the same.

> *"When I stand before thee at the day's end, thou shalt see my*
> *scars and know that I had my wounds and also my healing."*
> ~ Rabindranath Tagore[51]

WHISPERS OF THE HEART:

1. The question that must be answered is this: has your suffering been of benefit to you? Search for the meaning of your pain. Suffering is a natural facet of life. If you come to accept the lessons suffering has to offer and use them purposefully, painful encounters can become a fertile environment for growth that propels you onto the next plateau of your transcendent journey toward enlightenment. Change your thought about what you consider a negative experience.

2. If you can discover the *why's* of your life, you can bear any circumstance. Find a reason to persevere through the darkness. Set goals. This will allow you to rise to a place of higher

consciousness where as Lao Tzu describes, "rhinoceroses have no place to horn you."

3. Suffering is not a punishment. To the contrary, it is a gift from God, a tool from which to gain great wisdom. Try petitioning God to bless your suffering in a way that it might be purposeful to others. Ask yourself: how can I serve others? How do I most effectively assist those who are suffering? How can I help others in their quest to find peace within their agony, to find beauty in the belly of the beast?

CHAPTER 15

SUFFERING WITNESSED FROM THE PERSPECTIVE OF THE SOUL

Every human being is the author of his own
health or disease.
~ Swami Sivananda

For many years, I practiced within mainstream medicine. I thought I was helping *cure* my patients of cardiac maladies. It would take me years to realize my mistake.

I have since learned that there is a huge difference between *curing* a medical condition and actually participating in the process of *healing.* Curing utilizes evidence-based medicine that science provides, all of which has been generated in the mind. *Healing,* on the other hand, occurs in a place of much higher consciousness.

When our son, Tyler, sustained a severe spinal cord injury, so many well-intentioned people I knew and thousands of individuals I had never met began praying that Tyler would walk again.

My prayer was different from most. I prayed for our son's *healing.* I didn't have the audacity to suggest to God what I thought Tyler's healing should look like. I accepted that it wouldn't necessarily mean he'd walk again, but I did know that it would somehow involve the reconnection of his fractured body to his brilliant mind and beautiful soul.

One of my most formidable challenges has been convincing our son that his healing will come from within—that healing isn't in regaining the ability to walk; it's in coming to appreciate why walking again is unimportant in the overall scheme of things.

A while back, I awoke in the middle of the night and peeked into Tyler's bedroom to find him also wide-awake. It was 3 a.m., and we were both up, so we began talking. In the course of our conversation, Tyler posed a question to me that was so poignant in how he crafted the query. He asked me, "Pops, if you could choose to be anyone else in the world and move anywhere in the world you'd like, and no one would know you made the choice, where would you want to go, and who would you have join you?"

I shared with my son that recently I had been experiencing the feeling that everything seemingly was caving in on me. I told Ty that I felt like Davy Crockett at the Alamo and when I turned around to see who had my back, I realized I was alone with no one there to help me.

I remembered thinking: *I wish I could just run away from home.* But then I wondered, *where would I go? And who would I want to join me?*

I shared with Tyler that it didn't take me long to realize that as much un-fun as our current circumstance was, I realized that I wouldn't want to be anyone else, nor would I wish to move anywhere else. It was then I realized I was right where I was supposed to be, experiencing precisely what my soul needed in order to grow and expand its awareness.

With his gaze fixed on something off in the distance, Tyler offered, "I'm glad you said that, Pops, because I feel the same way."

Those were the most powerfully comforting words I could ever have hoped would come from Tyler. My prayer for the grace of God's healing for our son had been answered.

For the longest time, I had been so concerned that Tyler wouldn't be able to get beyond the all-consuming anger phase that, for him, had lasted over four years. Up to that point, his negative emotions and energy had kept him stuck in an inescapable quagmire that usurped from him any healing potential that might be available.

Early into my medical school training, I recognized the important role energy plays in our physical as well as spiritual wellbeing. Negative energy not only results in the manifestation of physical illness or injury, but it also impedes recovery. Positive energy, on the other hand, plays a critical role in the maintenance of the healthful state while fostering the process of healing.

It's not necessary to extricate the negative aspects from the mix; it's much more important to invite in the positive because it's in that milieu of constructive energy that true healing occurs. It's within the place of positive thoughts that we can learn to appreciate what we have rather than lamenting what we don't.

Knowing Tyler has reached the phase of acceptance of the death of part of his body, I am at peace, comforted in knowing that our son has begun to heal.

THE MOST PROFOUND LESSON OFFERED TO ME has come from the triumvirate described in chapter ten. The mortal self has physical limits. It is an ego trapped inside a transitory body. It's fragile and can be irreversibly altered by disease, injury, and even by our own thoughts.

The second member of the triad is death. It simply observes and waits patiently.

The third partner is the immortal self, the spiritual self that spends most of its time in a place of much higher consciousness.

My self that resides in the physical world undeniably feels the excruciating pain of a dad watching as his son endures immeasurable agony. My response to the suffering has been to become transparent, losing the solid aspect of myself. In the process, I have learned how to jettison the heavy payload of pain. It is from such a transcendent perch that I am able to watch my son progress on his path of healing.

I do so with no interference. It is in this place as a passive observer that my own spiritual growth has been unfolding as well. This, my dear gentles, is a place of unfathomable peace.

I have come to understand what Ram Dass meant:

"The saving grace is being able to witness suffering
from the perspective of the soul."[52]

WHISPERS OF THE HEART:

1. Be cognizant of the deleterious effects negative energy can create. Not only does it result in the manifestation of physical illness and injury, but negative energy also impedes recovery. Positive energy, on the other hand, plays a critical role in the maintenance of the healthful state while also fostering the process of healing. Especially in today's world with its excesses, dis-ease occurs when the delicate balance in life is lost. Try to recall how terrible such an imbalance feels when negativity overwhelms you. Now, consider how marvelous it is to live a life of equilibrium driven instead by positive energy. Your choice!

2. Try to spend as much time as you can on the transcendent perch of higher awareness. While there, you'll find no need to judge and no need to interfere. It is a peaceful place where you can simply draw from the experience whatever it is you choose. It is from the perch of such objectivity that you can witness suffering and death, all the while feeling no pain or sadness. Instead, you experience such distress from the perspective of the soul.

3. To paraphrase Mundaka Upanishad:

   Like three birds of golden plumage, inseparable
   companions, the individual physical self, its death, and
   the immortal Self are perched on the same branch
   of the tree. The material Self tastes of the sweet and
   bitter fruits of the tree. Savoring its perceived power,
   physical death threatens finality to life. But the
   immortal Self, tasting of neither ... calmly observes.

CHAPTER 16

UNFURLED BY THE DAWN

Your vision will become clear only when you can look into your own heart. Who looks outside, dreams; who looks inside, awakes.

~ Carl Jung

Many of us troll through life in a trance-like fashion, unaware of what is really transpiring. We don't have the time, or perhaps more accurately, we don't take the time to reflect on what life and death are really about. With such a limited mindset, a lifetime of experiences can end up offering only a confluence of consecutive moments that advance no cohesive comprehension.

Have you seriously contemplated the purpose of our being? Is our objective to become successful, crafting a legacy to leave behind? Or is our goal to be here simply to enjoy the experience? Might our purpose be to serve by touching the lives of others?

I believe the endgame for our being is perhaps much more significant than any of those listed above. The point for our existence here is to grow, to mature, and to progress on our individual spiritual path.

Transformative enlightenment is what this is all about. Transformative enlightenment is when we cultivate our consciousness in such a way that it results in a shift in the paradigm of thought. Such a shift will lead us to change not only the way we think, it will also modify what we say and what we do and ultimately it will change what it is we are to become.

For most, such an ever-expanding awareness likely begins long before we become cognizant of it. We're like a seed that has been sewn, but has yet to sprout.

All too often as life is being lived, our soul becomes vastly undernourished while we attend to the physical world and its many perceived obligations. The responsibility for providing financial security, a safe environment, and sustenance require an emphasis on the material world that unfortunately puts our spiritual yearnings for truth and knowledge on the back burner.

During my busy career as a cardiologist, I recall far too many times pausing to reflect amidst the chaos of my chosen profession. I promised myself on more occasions than I'd like to admit that once I achieved certain goals, then I'd finally take the time to attend to the spiritual aspects of my life.

But what does such procrastination bring? At the end of our time on Earth, all too often we sadly realize we have busied our precious time away, having never gotten around to nurturing our spiritual self, the most important facet we have.

Once the decision is made to embark upon our transcendent journey, the path may lead us through desolate terrain where there is barely enough oxygen to sustain life.

In *Awakening the Buddha Within,* Surya Das shares:

> *"When you are going through the barren deserts or fearsome
> minefields of what Saint John of the Cross called the 'dark night
> of the soul,' doubt and healthy skepticism are not just obstacles,
> they are also the propellant that fuels the spiritual engine."*[53]

The journey will take time. We must remain patient. The "I want it and I want it now" attitude many of us have leaves us frustrated when we realize enlightenment isn't something immediately achievable. In fact, it isn't something we can achieve at all. It's an awareness that evolves as the conditions for its unfolding ripen.

The more aggressively enlightenment is pursued, the greater will be the struggle to align with it. When a seedling is planted, all the coaxing imaginable will not cause the tree to grow any faster than the Universe allows. So too it is with enlightenment. It might be that we need to live many years before a lesson we are to learn presents itself. On the other hand, the wisdom of a thousand tutorials might be imparted to us in just a blink of the eye.

Enlightenment, when it occurs, advances spontaneously. It doesn't involve any effort on our part. In fact, it's quite the opposite. By its very nature, we cannot acquire spiritual consciousness. Such awareness begins to unfold once profound messages begin to comfortably settle in to the deep recesses of the soul and are recognized. All we must do is simply listen to the brilliant silence the Universe offers.

MOST OF US HAVE DIFFICULTY BELIEVING WHAT WE CANNOT SEE. Imagine being in a huge, darkened warehouse. The only thing we have to illuminate our way is a small flashlight that can only show us what is directly in its diminutive beam. As we stumble through the darkness, we might catch a glimpse of some things, but there will be many objects in close proximity that remain unseen simply because the flashlight isn't strong enough to reveal them. But the fact that we can't see them doesn't mean they're not there.

If the overhead lights of the storeroom were to be suddenly turned on, in an instant everything in the vast space would come into full view. Once seen, the clarity of the gift en*light*enment has offered cannot be taken away from us. It would feel like the moment of exhilaration when a jetliner, surrounded in the thickness of gray clouds, suddenly eclipses the edge of the cloud coverage and bursts into the wild blue yonder of clear skies above where all is seen.

Despite its seeming limitation, darkness has critically important qualities. Every tree grows in two directions. Its branches extend upward toward the radiant sun while spreading its taproots into the darkness of the soil. As much as the light enriches us, we also gain spiritual nourishment from the darkness as well.

Enlightenment may come from a guru, a friend, or a total stranger. From wherever it arises and without judgment accept it.

Appreciate the offering, remembering that each of us is the Divine in camouflage. Every lesson sent our way is God-given. We should be open to learn from everyone and everything we encounter, exalting in the diversity of the deliverer. We shouldn't be dissuaded by anyone's religious affiliation or what belief systems they have or have not embraced. It's not the tradition or law that counts, it's the spiritual wisdom offered that is of paramount importance.

In order to truly awaken, we must spiritualize everything, every day, and everywhere. As the dawn unfurls and the darkness recedes, take the time and listen to what the wind has to say as it sighs. Savor the white noise during a walk in the rain. In the woods, there is no better place to connect with the Source of All than while immersed in the cloak of nature.

Shhh … Listen.

WHISPERS OF THE HEART:

1. Contemplate our purpose for being here. Is our reason for being—superficial, or is our objective for being here to grow, to mature, to progress on what is our unique spiritual path? Silence is the guide to our inner self where we will rediscover all that has been forgotten.

2. Transformative Enlightenment is what life is all about. We should groom our consciousness in such a way that it results in a shift in the way we think. As my dear friend Wayne Dyer was known for saying: "When you change the way you look at things, those things you look at will change." In the process, notice the dramatic difference in what it is you are becoming.

3. In order to truly awaken, we must spiritualize everything, every day, and everywhere.

CHAPTER 17
REINCARNATION OF THE SOUL

How does one become a butterfly?
You must want to fly so much
that you are willing to give up being a caterpillar.
~ Trina Paulus

E ach of our souls is like an eagle soaring high above Mother Earth. Every so often, swooping down from its majestic place in the heavens, the soul joins the activities of the world, if only briefly. It then ascends once again, circling between incarnations.

I have often contemplated the perplexing thought of whether I have lived a previous life, and if I have, why can't I remember it? Does my amnesia mean that I've never had a past life?

I must admit there are many experiences I don't recall. I have no memory of what I did on my 14th birthday or what I was feeling the day before 9-11. I would imagine those experiences were vivid at the time, and just because I can't remember the specifics today doesn't mean they didn't happen. If I have forgotten so many distinct moments of my current life, it is certainly conceivable that I could have also forgotten what happened in a previous one.

I agree with Voltaire, who once said: *"After all, it is no more surprising to me to be born twice than it is to be born once."*

If we embrace the belief of reincarnation, we accept the premises that both time and space are limitless. No longer are we shackled by linear time with the sand in the hourglass steadily marking the passage of moments that can never be retrieved.

Believers of reincarnation acknowledge that some part of an individual's essence, likely the soul, continues and ultimately is reintroduced into another physical being. With such an expanded view of life, there is a calmness to be had knowing that a particular lifetime isn't the only one we will encounter.

Many consider reincarnation to be exclusively associated with Eastern religions, but societies that embrace reincarnation span the globe. As an example, predating the influence Christianity had on them, Native Americans' concept of the soul and reincarnation was well developed. They believe that the human soul exists prior to birth and can be reborn again and again. An intriguing belief is that a single soul has the potential to be reincarnated in more than one person at the same time!

Several years ago, I experienced what I believe was a single soul that inhabited two sentient beings concurrently. After our son's spinal cord injury, we spent four months in Denver as he underwent physical rehabilitation.

One morning as I was walking briskly to my car, I came upon a little old lady who was shuffling at a snail's pace on the sidewalk. She was hunched over as she walked, and her chin was frozen in a severely flexed position that allowed her to see only by lifting her eyes to the top of her eye sockets. Six plastic bags full of groceries weighed her down. She had already shuffled for more than three blocks from the local grocery store.

She wore tattered, threadbare clothing and a straw fishing hat over her gray hair to protect her eyes from the glare of the early Denver sun. I whisked past her on my mission to run a quick errand before Tyler awakened.

I had gotten to my car, turned on the ignition, and cranked up the air conditioner when I was suddenly struck by a thought: *I don't really have it that bad. I'm able to walk to my car without difficulty. I'm sitting in an air-conditioned vehicle, protected from the heat. I'm able to go anywhere I wish in safety and comfort. I have plenty of food and clothing.* And then it hit me that I had just thoughtlessly blasted past an unfortunate elderly woman who would struggle for God knows how many more blocks in the 85-degree weather, carrying her cumbersome load home.

I put the car in gear and turned in the opposite direction of my destination. I drove back to the spot where I had last seen her, but she was gone. I drove around for a few minutes until I found her walking up a rather steep hill on one of the side streets. Her movements were decidedly more sluggish now. I pulled the car up to her and got out, approaching her from behind.

"Excuse me, ma'am, may I help you?" I asked.

She slowly turned around and with a broad, partially toothless smile, she musically responded, "Oh, no. I'm doing just fine! But thank you, sir, for your kind offer."

She had the most beautiful hazel eyes I had ever seen; I became mesmerized by her gaze. As we looked into each other's eyes, I felt an immediate connection, a familiarity with her. Her entire essence smiled through those eyes, her radiance revealing to me a beautiful soul. She added, "God bless you, child."

I turned to walk away. Taking a few steps, I paused and looked back at her and smiled. She had resumed her journey, shuffling along the pavement. It amazed me that I had come upon a person for whom I had been feeling sympathy and sorrow. And *she* was blessing *me*. I was envious, wanting to attain the peace and fortitude this woman had. She could have very easily accepted my offer of assistance and ridden in the comfort of my air-conditioned car for the duration of her trip back home. Instead, she chose to continue along her path, arduous as it was.

As I watched her walk away, the proverb, "But for the grace of God go I," scrolled through my mind. I was thinking that were it not for God's grace, it could be me carrying those burdensome bags, struggling to walk uphill on this oppressively hot and humid day.

Then the strangest thing happened. As she walked away, I could have sworn I heard her say, "But for the grace of God go I."

It wasn't until eight months later, back at home in Ohio, that I was gently awakened in the middle of the night by the image of this elderly woman's smiling face, her radiant eyes gazing into mine. In the middle of the night, I realized that I had gazed into those eyes before. She shared the same gorgeous hazel eyes with Art Blair, my heart patient, dear friend, and mentor I have mentioned in this book.

The following morning, I called Art and asked him if I might come over for a visit. When I arrived at his trailer home, we hugged. Not letting go of the embrace, I held his arms, peering into his eyes for a very long time. He responded in kind. As I looked deeply into the portals to his soul, what I saw astounded me. Both his soul and the beautiful soul of the lady I met on the streets of Denver appeared to be one and the same!

When I shared with him my observation and asked if he thought it preposterous to think that one soul could inhabit two bodies at the same time, Art just smiled. His gorgeous hazel eyes glimmered in affirmation at the possibility. It had been his suggestion to me years before that I be open to everything, attached to nothing. I was now practicing that as my enlightenment took yet another step forward!

IN ITS CAVERNOUS DEPTHS, THE OCEAN IS UNIFORM, similar in its makeup, consistent in its calmness. In contrast, as one looks across the sea's windswept surface, the turbulence of many waves can be seen. Some swells are quite large; other waves are barely perceptible.

The vast ocean is water and the wave is water. They differ only in form. Although each whitecap may appear to be separate, in truth, there is no individuation. After all, a wave is nothing more than the ocean pushing up on itself. There is no difference between the edge of the wave and its deepest manifestation. The two are never disconnected from one another.

When a wave loses its waveness, where does it go? Its inertia doesn't die. It simply blends back into its source, the ocean, as it has since time immemorial. Neither its birth nor its death is possible.

So it is with us as well. Like the wave, our essence doesn't lose its inertia when we move on to the next phase of life. We don't die.

Striving to be like the waves, we too realize that our nature is that of no beginning and no end.

And because we are no more separated from God than the mist is from the ocean, it's not necessary for us to embark on a circuitous journey in search of a connection with the Source of Our Creation. That bond already exists.

If I were to pose the question to the Great Architect of the Universe: "Hey God, where are you anyway?" I wouldn't be surprised by the response: "Why, I am here in front of you. Can't you see me? I am behind you. I am standing to your right and beside you on your left. I am below you, above you, and most assuredly, I am within you. Where else could I be?"

God *is* in everything that is, whether revealed in form or manifested as formless. The essence of this Divine Source is interwoven in harmonious fashion with every person, with all plants, with every single animal, and every object. None is more precious than any other because we are all comprised of the same elements. Everything is a piece of God.

As it emerges from its Source, the soul is like a bead of water in the turbulence of a breaking wave crashing into a boulder-strewn shore. The droplet is thrust upward into and surrounded by air as the process of evaporation occurs. Sooner or later, that droplet will join with others in the same phase, condense, and rejoin the ocean as rain.

This is precisely what occurs when a soul leaves Source, transforming to become a spiritual being having a temporary human experience. In this manifestation, the soul provides a vital function serving as an extension of the Divine in physical form. Each soul wears spiritual attire that differs from what any other soul has ever adorned. It has a unique purpose for reincarnating as well. The soul has purpose, not only for its own growth and evolution but also for the benefit of the entire Universe.

How the soul departs the body varies from spirit to spirit. Some leave right away; others delay their separation. There's a sweet story about an elderly man who transitioned. His soul separated, lifting from the vessel, and began to depart. But at the last moment, it looked back fondly at the vessel that had accompanied it for 84 years. The soul then turned back and sat next to the dead body, thanking it for the wonderful service it had provided. When the spirit rose to depart, it leaned over and kissed the old man good-bye.

WHISPERS OF THE HEART:

1. Are there times when you feel separated from God? Envision yourself as a tiny droplet of rain simply blending back into its source, the ocean. This is how each of us, as an integral part of the whole, rejoins the sea of the Divine.

2. Like water that settles into low places, be humble. You are not any more special than anything else God has created. Everything is an expression of God and should be revered as such.

3. By passing on to others the good and beautiful aspects of your essence, you can be reborn long before you take your last breath. In doing so, immortality is yours!

CHAPTER 18

A GOOD DAY TO DIE

If we have been pleased with life, we should not be displeased
with death, since it comes from the hand of the same master.
~ Michelangelo

Along the journey of discovering how to confront our own mortality, we must also come to terms with how we have lived our lives as well. There are many accounts of individuals who on the brink of death undergo their life review. The experience recalls to consciousness all the memories of their most recent incarnation as well as any past conflicts yet to be resolved.

But wouldn't it be more enriching and even more productive to have a lifetime during which to review our missteps and accomplishments? Or stated differently, wouldn't it be marvelous to wake up before we die?

As a medical intern, I was forever changed by an experience of participating in an exhausting resuscitation. When our attempts to revive the man failed, the attending physician pronounced the patient dead.

As all of those involved in the futile exercise left the patient's hospital room, I hung around for a few moments, reflecting on what had just transpired. On the gurney was a dead man who just 45 minutes ago had been alive. Looking at his now lifeless corpse, I came to a stark realization that at some point, I'll be a cadaver lying on a gurney with some newbie intern staring at me, wondering what this thing called life is all about.

For years, I reflected on my own finiteness. Apprehensive about how my death might unfold, I pondered what disease would ultimately get me and whether my demise would be sudden or one of those slow, excruciatingly painful experiences.

I tried to imagine what my final moments would be like. Would chaos and turmoil envelop me as I departed, or might I be blessed enough to settle into a peaceful transition?

Up to that point, my life had been about making plans. I wasted so much precious time not concentrating on the here and now, instead fretting about the future. I carefully mapped out the arc of my career path as best I could, and developed a financial plan that I hoped would guarantee security for my family, were I to die young.

Despite such material preparation, I remained concerned that my death might blindside me, leaving me totally unprepared spiritually.

One of the first challenges I faced in dealing with the fear of mortality was learning how not to take my own death too personally. Once I grew to accept that my demise would be a natural event, I came to appreciate death's intricate connection with life. The reality is that God presents a life cycle that includes what we refer to as death.

Some religions believe that we choose when we are to be born into a particular lifetime, what we'll experience, and when we are to exit. In between the two bookends of birth and death ensues a battle of wits, so to speak. Close to the end, when the struggle seems to intensify between the body's will to continue living and the soul's decision to depart, the soul exercises its veto power. A peaceful moment eventually comes when the struggle ends and with peaceful surrender, life leaves the body. This is an energetic phenomenon, not acquiescence or throwing in the towel out of weakness. This is about the strength of the spirit deciding the time has come to let go of the vessel.

Each of us inherits a finite amount of energy from our ancestors to utilize throughout our lifetime. Small amounts of this *chi*, the energy force of life as described in Chinese medicine, is the fuel we consume each day. If we're cautious not to overuse our energy stores, some of this battery pack can be replenished. But when our energy stores become completely depleted, the exhaustion of our lifespan occurs, and death ensues. When this moment is reached, it is manifest as a last burst. There remains no essence left behind in the vessel and at this point, the body collapses into itself.

I experienced such a phenomenon during my medical school training. A middle-aged lady was admitted to the Intensive Care Unit after having suffered a massive brain hemorrhage. Despite an extremely poor prognosis, her family was hesitant to end the heroic measures that were keeping her alive. After many days without any signs of improvement, they finally realized the hopelessness of her situation and agreed to let her go.

She was on no medications to sedate or paralyze her, yet she had not moved a muscle since her admission. From the medical perspective, she had been neurologically dead for well over two weeks.

Those of us who had worked with her every day had become very attached to her, admiring her tenacity and perseverance. When the time came for the ventilator to be turned off, her family and some of the medical staff couldn't bear to be present when she ultimately died.

As we disconnected her from life support, my interest in cardiology compelled me to listen with my stethoscope to her dying heart. I leaned over the bed and began listening intently to what would be the final contractions of her heart.

After three to four minutes, her heart rate began slowing down until her heart ceased beating altogether. It was a very peaceful passing … that is, until she suddenly sat up and wrapped her arms around my shoulders. It was then that she exhaled one last breath that seemed to last forever. Then her entire body relaxed back down on the bed, and she moved no more.

I remained in her room, looking at her for a very long time, trying to understand what had just transpired. To my eye, her frail body appeared to have caved into itself.

Her embrace of me was extremely perplexing. Had she hugged me as a gesture of gratitude for the care I had helped provide her? Was she thanking me for freeing up the mortal coils that would enable her to continue her journey back to Source? Whatever the explanation, her embrace touched me deeply.

We are all placed here on this earth with a purpose. Each of our lives has a mission, one that might impact thousands of lives or, just as importantly, might change the course of only one. When our mission is complete, we move on. I know in preparing for my own death, whenever that may occur, I have gained invaluable insight I pray will help others navigate their journey.

As I have grown through experience, I have learned how to make friends with death. It's a process that can't be rushed and may take a lifetime to achieve. I believe that as I plan in earnest for a death that is meaningful, when the time comes for my transition, I will be free to soar to the next plateau. I also know that if I allow myself to be anchored to any negative aspects of life, the strongest wings imaginable won't be able to lift me up into flight.

If we are in the right state of mind, the moment of death can be a powerfully purifying experience from the perspective of Karma. This final mindset is of utmost importance as positive attitudes and energy propel us to a more positive rebirthing experience. In comparison, if our last moments are filled with turmoil and agitation, rebirth will likely be unenviably negative.

The last thoughts and emotions we experience before we die have an extremely powerful effect on our immediate future. *"So as you think, so shall you be"* has never been truer than it is in this context.

HOW DO I WANT TO DIE? Some feel they must leave this world in much the same way they entered it, kicking and screaming. Others choose to make their transition a peaceful one.

As I write this, two individuals immediately come to mind. Both suffered from the same malady. The first was one of the founding physicians of a medical school in the Midwest. He was quite debilitated with congestive heart failure. I remember being taken aback by his anger as he faced his infirmity. I would have thought having a successful career in medicine and watching a medical school flourish that he helped to create would have given him solace for a life well lived.

Instead, he lashed out at anyone who came in close proximity to his cubicle in the ICU. On this particular night, I was a second-year medical student on call in the hospital. When I heard the Code Blue called over the intercom, I ran to the ICU to observe the resuscitation attempt about to unfold.

The elderly physician was in extremis with his vital organs failing. A team of healthcare providers rushed to his room. It was obvious even to this student that his prognosis was extremely poor.

Going in and out of consciousness and with a thick tongue, he barked out orders to the staff. Incredibly, he was attempting to run his own Code Blue!

The last words to cross his lips were: "Damn it, doctor, I told you to give me more bicarb!" And then he died.

I recall thinking how sad to be at the threshold of one's life ending and to taint the experience with such anger. He would not be the last patient I'd see battling the Angel of Death to the death.

The other patient who comes to mind approached his impending crossing in a diametrically opposed fashion. After several major heart attacks, Jim too suffered from congestive heart failure. His heart was beating at 15 percent capacity. He was extremely fatigued and short of breath at rest and experienced significant difficulty taking just a few steps with legs so filled with fluid, they looked like they were ready to explode.

Jim had been admitted to the Coronary Care Unit (CCU) the previous evening. The following morning as I entered his room, he had a cardiac arrest. His heart had gone into a chaotic rhythm disturbance inconsistent with life. I shocked his heart within 15 seconds of the arrest and was able to stabilize him.

Over the course of the next six hours or so, his sick heart stopped beating effectively multiple times, each requiring another shock to restart it.

When yet another Code Blue was called, I was rounding on the ninth floor of the hospital. After running down to the CCU on the second floor, I ran breathlessly into Jim's room. By the time I arrived, he'd already received three shocks from a defibrillator, and his bed was angled in the head-down position in order to facilitate greater blood flow to his brain.

As I approached him, Jim looked up at me and asked, "Terry, how's your day going?"

Now, here's a guy who has already tried to die multiple times that day, and he's wondering how *my* day was going!

I shared with him that my day was going just fine and thanked him for his concern. I then revealed to him what he already knew—that his situation was dire. I also explained that with his terribly weakened heart, there wasn't much else I could offer. Despite that declaration, I conveyed to him that if he chose to continue, I would do whatever possible to help sustain his life.

His wife was seated next to the head of the bed, holding his hand, gently caressing it as we spoke. Jim turned to his wife and as if trying to decide which movie to go see at the theater, he calmly asked her, "Well Hon, what do you think we should do?"

What transpired was simply beautiful as this loving couple that had shared over 60 years together calmly and openly discussed the most momentous decision of their lives. They agreed to halt any further heroics. The two lovebirds conjoined forever entered the next phase of their lives—at peace.

That's how I want to die! I don't want to be in turmoil as the door to infinity opens for me. I want to be at peace, just like Jim and his loving wife.

I don't want my death to fill my loved ones or myself with sadness. I want Patch Adams at my bedside, clowning around and making me laugh. Because if I can experience my transition to the other side of life with a grin on my face and a positive attitude, I have no doubt my crossing will be an event of beauty. I'll be able to continue unencumbered, knowing well that I'll be on my way to reconvening with the Master of the Universe.

Death isn't the end. It facilitates the continuation of consciousness that has become detached from the physical body. It's threshold opens into a limitless realm.

I think this is what will ultimately happen to me: When it's my turn to transition, losing the solid aspect of myself, I will become transparent. Letting go of the attachment to the limitations of this material world, I will rise above the resistance, transcending to a place of much higher awareness. It will be from this perch that I will passively watch ... as my physical self dies.

I am certain some might read these words and suggest that thinking so much about death and dying is morbid and depressing. For me, it is quite the opposite. Anticipating the future, wherever that might be and in whatever form it may manifest, is not depressing at all. It is absolutely exhilarating!

EPILOGUE

BEYOND THE AVALANCHE
OF SILENCE

A drianne was a delightful 82-year-old. I was privileged to serve as her cardiologist for well over a decade. From the moment I assumed her care, we connected. We were both raised in the South. She was from Charleston, South Carolina; I was from Louisville, Kentucky. We had much in common.

She had a very serious heart condition that required the placement of an implantable defibrillator, a device that would save her life by shocking her out of a life-threatening heart rhythm disturbance should it occur.

One morning, she presented to the hospital with her defibrillator shocking her repetitively. Despite my efforts to quiet her heart, she continued to receive jolts of electric shocks by the device. By the end of the day, it had delivered over 85 shocks, sadly all of them while she remained fully awake—a very painful circumstance.

Late that afternoon, she beckoned me to her room. As I entered, she said, "You know Terry, I'm not afraid to die. I've actually been dying for ten years now."

I responded by saying, "No, Adrianne, you've had a great ten years! You have actually done so much better than I ever expected."

She then added, "What I meant by that was I have been preparing for my death for over a decade. I have been consciously shedding all the extraneous things most people consider so important. I do not fear death, Terry," she said resolutely. "But, I don't wish to continue living like this any longer. Will you turn my defibrillator off?"

I told her that of course I would if that was her wish, explaining that the next time her heart degenerated into a chaotic rhythm, she would cross over. She understood the implications of her decision.

I felt sad for her as she was facing such a momentous decision by herself. Her children and their families all lived in South Carolina. They were unified in their resolve not to allow their loved one to endure any more unnecessary pain. As circumstances would dictate, they would not be able to make it to her bedside until the following day. The unanimous decision was made to go ahead and deactivate her defibrillator.

I shared with Adrianne what a privilege it had been for me to care for her all these years and what a special friend she had been to me. As I turned to leave the room, she hesitantly added, "You know Terry, I have one more request." She paused for a moment, looked up at me, and with a tear in her eye, asked, "Will you hold my hand?"

I sat down beside her on the bed. We hugged. Smiling, I replied, "Adrianne, of course I'll hold your hand ... as long as you don't tell my wife. She gets very jealous when I hold hands with beautiful women!" I winked at her.

I shared with her the honor I felt being there with her at this important moment of her life. Once I turned the defibrillator off, I asked the nurse to leave us alone in the room. Adrianne and I sat there together, hand in hand. We reminisced about southern living, and as we spoke, I caressed her hand; she responded to mine in kind. This time we shared together was precious.

I looked up at her heart monitor at the precise moment her heart stopped beating. Her eyes fluttered for a moment and then gently rolled back as she peacefully transitioned.

While I sat there in silence, I continued holding her hand, looking at it. I realized that it was the same hand I had been holding just a split second before, yet now it was no longer responsive to mine. Still warm, her hand had within its veins the same blood cells and electrolytes. The same ligaments remained; its bony structure hadn't changed. It was the same hand, except for one thing—the spirit had left the vessel.

The strangest thought crossed my mind. I recalled the movie *ET.* There is a scene where ET is showing off to the little boy in his bedroom. When ET's bony finger reaches over and touches a flower... *ding,* the flower immediately withers. As he touches it again, *ding,* the flower comes back to life.

It occurred to me what had just happened to Adrianne. God had *dinged* her. And in that instant, her spirit left the vessel she had called home for over eighty years. For the first time in my career, because I allowed myself to do so, I could feel her energy swirling behind me in the room. It hovered for only a moment, and then, *whoooosh,* it was gone!

We think we know so much about science. The truth is, we do not. But there is one fact we do know for certain. Energy doesn't die. It transforms; it changes. And when its stint in a particular form is done, it offers itself back to the Universe where that energy will be forever.

From the moment Adrianne's spirit departed her body, her energy, her essence, her soul, set sail on its journey to infinity. Accepting that premise, I believe it is equally true that her soul existed for infinity *before* she was dinged into her worldly vessel.

Considering ad infinitum on either side of what we call life, the time we spend here is infinitesimal. This is not meant to minimize the experience, as the time we are here is neither inconsequential nor insignificant. It matters not whether the span of our life lasts four days, four weeks, four decades, or fourscore. It is in the relative sense, fleeting.

Liberation rests in the acceptance that there is no annihilation. We don't die; we transform. In acknowledging that Truth, we come to accept the process without trepidation, celebrating our transition as one of the most miraculous adventures of life.

Death is not our enemy; it is our companion, our guide, our friend. Death reunites us with eternity, where there is *no beginning... and no end.*

My dear gentles,

Thank you for joining me on this journey toward enlightenment. I trust you have learned as much from the experience as I have. I am grateful our Bumper Cars caressed one another.

Namaste,

Dr. Terry Gordon

RECOMMENDED READING

A Brief Guide to Beliefs, Ideas, Theologies, Mysteries, and Movements by Linda Edwards (Westminster John Knox Press, 2001)

A Lifetime of Wisdom: Embracing the Way God Heals You by Joni Eareckson Tada (Zondervan, 2009)

Anam Cara: A Book of Celtic Wisdom by John O'Donohue (HarperCollins, 1997)

Being Mortal: Medicine and What Matters in the End by Atul Gawande (Metropolitan Books, 2014)

"Born Toward Dying" by Father Richard John Neuhaus (*First Things* Journal, 2000)

Does The Soul Survive? A Jewish Journey to Belief in Afterlife, Past Lives & Living with Purpose by Rabbi Elie Kaplan Spitz (Jewish Lights Publishing, 2000)

Facing Death and Finding Hope: A Guide to the Emotional and Spiritual Care of the Dying by Christine Longaker (Doubleday, 1997)

Life After Life by Raymond A. Moody Jr., MD (Bantam Books, 1975)

Living the Wisdom of the Tao: The Complete Tao Te Ching and Affirmations by Dr. Wayne W. Dyer (Hay House, 2008)

Making Loss Matter: Creating Meaning in Difficult Times by Rabbi David Wolpe (Riverhead Trade, 2000)

90 Minutes In Heaven: A True Story of Death & Life by Don Piper with Cecil Murphy (Fleming H. Revell, 2004)

No Death, No Fear: Comforting Wisdom for Life by Thich Nhat Hanh (Riverhead Books, 2002)

Nurturing Healing Love: A Mother's Journey of Hope and Forgiveness by Scarlett Lewis with Natasha Stoynoff (Hay House, 2013)

On Grief & Grieving: Finding the Meaning of Grief Through the Five Stages of Loss by Elisabeth Kübler-Ross, MD and David A. Kessler, MD (Scribner, 2005)

Reflections On Life After Life by Raymond A. Moody Jr., MD (Bantam Books, 1977)

Saved by the Light by Dannion Brinkley with Paul Perry (Villard Books, 1994 & Harper Torch, 1995)

Staring at the Sun: Overcoming the Terror of Death by Irvin D. Yalom (Jossey-Bass, 2008)

Still Here: Embracing Aging, Changing, and Dying by Ram Dass (The Penguin Group, 2000)

Talking To Heaven: A Medium's Message of Life After Death by James Van Praagh (The Penguin Group, 1997)

The Book of Secrets: Unlocking the Hidden Dimensions of Your Life by Deepak Chopra (Harmony Books, 2004)

The Deeper Wound: Recovering the Soul from Fear and Suffering by Deepak Chopra (Harmony Books, 2001)

The Tibetan Book of the Dead: Liberation Through Understanding In the Between, translated by Robert F. Thurman (Bantam Books, 1994)

The Tunnel and the Light: Essential Insights on Living and Dying by Elisabeth Kübler-Ross, MD (Marlowe & Company, 1999)

Why Faith Matters by Rabbi David Wolpe (HarperCollins, 2008)

Your Sacred Self: Making the Decision to Be Free by Dr. Wayne W. Dyer (HarperCollins, 1995)

One River, Many Wells: Wisdom Springing From Global Faiths by Mathew Fox (Penguin Putnam, 2000)

Cover artwork by Britt Gordon Blasdell
www.brittgordonart.com

NOTES

1   Jeff Levin, "The discourse of faith and medicine: a tale of two literatures," *Theoretical Medicine and Bioethics,* July 31, 2018, https://doi.org/10.1007/s11017-018-9449-9.

2   Jeff Levin, *God, Faith, and Health* (New York: John Wiley, 2002).

3   Larry Dossey, MD, *Space, Time & Medicine* (Boston: Shambhala; New Science Library, 1982).

4   Larry Dossey, MD, *One Mind: How Our Individual Mind Is Part of a Greater Consciousness and Why It Matters* (Carlsbad, CA: Hay House, 2013).

5   Carl Jung, quoted in *Jung on Death and Immortality, selected and introduced by Jenny Yates* (Princeton, NJ: Princeton University Press, 1999), 3.

6   Richard P. Sloan, PhD, Emilia Bagiella, PhD, Tia Powell, MD, "Religion, spirituality, and medicine," *The Lancet,* Feb 1999, 353(9153), 664-7.

7   Larry Dossey, MD, *Reinventing Medicine: Beyond Mind-Body to a New Era of Healing* (San Francisco, CA: HarperCollins, 1999).

8   Bob Rickard, "Interview with Ben Rock and Daniel Myrick," *Fortean Times,* November 1999, 128, 38-40.

9   Alfred Tennyson, from "Locksley Hall," quoted in *The Concise Oxford Dictionary of Quotations,* Angela Partington, ed. Third edition (New York: Oxford University Press, 1993), 326, no. 11.

10 Charlie Broad, quoted in *Parapsychology, Philosophy, and Spirituality,* David Ray Griffin (Albany, NY: SUNY Press, 1997), 98.

11 Karl Barth, quoted in *Parapsychology, Philosophy, and Spirituality,* David Ray Griffin (Albany, NY: SUNY Press, 1997), 146.

12 Bertrand Russell, quoted in *Immortality,* Paul Edwards, ed. (Amherst, NY: Prometheus Books, 1997), v.

13 Debra Denker, *Sisters on the Bridge of Fire* (Mission Hills, CA: Burning Gate Press, 1993), 318.

14 Colin McGinn, quoted in *Immortality,* Paul Edwards, ed. (Amherst, NY: Prometheus Books, 1997), 294.

15 John Searle, quoted on front cover of *Journal of Consciousness Studies,* 2, no.1, 1995.

16 Jerry Fodor, "The big idea," *The Times Literary Supplement,* July 3, 1992, 20.

17 John Maddox, "The Unexpected Science to Come," *Scientific American,* December 1999, 281(6), 62-67.

18 Donald Hoffman, "Consciousness and the mind-body problem," *Mind & Matter,* 2008, 6(1), 87-121.

19 Paul Davies, *Space and Time in the Modern Universe* (New York: Cambridge University Press, 1977), 221.

20 John Briggs and F. David Peat, "Interview with David Bohm," *Omni,* January 1987, 68ff.

21 David Ray Griffin, *Parapsychology, Philosophy, & Spirituality: A Postmodern Exploration* (Albany, NY: SUNY Press, 1997), 290-291.

22 Ibid.

23 Deepak Chopra, *Life After Death: The Burden of Proof* (New York: Harmony Books, 2006), 82.

24 Sogyal Rinpoche, *The Tibetan Book of Living and Dying* (San Francisco: HarperCollins, 1992), 33.

25 Sigmund Freud, *On the History of the Psycho-Analytic Moment* (London: The Hogarth Press, 1915).

26 Lao Tzu, *The Tao Te Ching,* Translated by Stephen Addiss & Stanley Lombardo (Boston: Shambhala Publications, 1993), 2nd Verse.

27 Carl Jung, *Musings of Carl Jung,* C. Sreechinth, ed. (UB Tech, 2018), 138.

28 Wayne W. Dyer, PhD, *Change Your Thoughts–Change Your Life: Living the Wisdom of the Tao* (Carlsbad, CA: Hay House, 2007), 243.

29 *Little Big Man.* 1970. Directed by Arthur Penn. Burbank, CA: Warner Brothers Pictures. DVD.

30 Ernest Hemingway referenced his NDE in a letter he wrote to his family while he was convalescing in Milan from a shrapnel wound, dated Oct.18, 1918. "Famous People on their Near-Death Experiences," Astral Institute.com, last modified January 3, 2015, http://astral-institute.com/famous-people-near-death-experiences/.

31 Carl Jung, *Memories, Dreams, Reflections* (New York: Vintage Books, 1989), 289-290.

32 Ibid.

33 Margot Grey, *Return From Death: An Exploration of the Near-Death Experience* (Boston and London: Arkana, 1985).

34 Kenneth Ring, *Life at Death: A Scientific Investigation of the Near-Death Experience* (New York: William Morrow, 1982).

35 Anita Moorjani, *Dying To Be Me: My Journey from Cancer, to Near Death, To True Healing* (Carlsbad, CA: Hay House, 2012), 142

36 Erwin W. Lutzer, *One Minute After You Die* (Chicago: Moody Publishers, 1997), 30-31.

37 Kenneth Patchen, *The Journal of Albion Moonlight* (New York: United Book Guild, 1941).

38 Paul P. Pearsall, PhD, Gary Schwartz, PhD, and Linda Russek, PhD, "Changes in Heart Transplant Recipients that Parallel the Personalities of Their Donors," *Integrative Medicine*, March 2000, 65-72.

39 don Miguel Ruiz, MD, *The Four Agreements* (San Rafael, CA: Amber-Allen Publishing, 1997).

40 don Miguel Ruiz, MD, *The Mastery of Love* (San Rafael, CA: Amber-Allen Publishing, 1999).

41 Gary Schwartz, PhD, with William Simon and Linda Russek, PhD, *The Afterlife Experiments: Breakthrough Scientific Evidence of Life After Death* (New York: Atria Books, 2003), 283-284.

42 Ibid, 285.

43 Michel de Montaigne, *The Complete Essays*, translated and edited by M.A. Screech (London: Allen Lane, 1991), 95.

44 Thich Nhat Hanh, quoted in *A Lifetime of Peace: Essential Writings by and about Thich Nhat Hanh,* Jennifer Schwamm Willis, ed. (New York: Marlow & Company, 2003).

45 Henry Ward Beecher, "Henry Ward Beecher Quotes," allauthors.com, (n.d.), https://allauthor.com/quote/1243/.

46 Bill Guggenheim and Judy Guggenheim, *Hello From Heaven* (New York: Bantam Books, 1996), 23-112.

47 Elisabeth Kübler-Ross, MD, *On Death & Dying* (New York: Macmillan, 1969).

48 Albert Pike, *Morals and Dogma of the Ancient and Accepted Scottish Rite of Freemasonry* (US: The Supreme Council for the Southern Jurisdiction of the United States, 1906).

49 Viktor Frankl, *Man's Search for Meaning* (New York: Simon & Schuster, 1959).

50 Emily Willen, "The Privilege of Pain," LLA Foundation, January 15, 2016, https://www.llafoundation.com/grief-as-a-teacher/. Reprinted with permission from the author.

51 Rabindranath Tagore, *Collected Poems and Plays of Rabindranath Tagore* (New York: The Macmillan Company, 1967).

52 Ram Dass, *Polishing the Mirror: How to Live from Your Spiritual Heart* (Boulder, CO: Sounds True, 2013).

53 Surya Das, *Awakening the Buddha Within* (New York: Broadway Books, 1997).

Made in the USA
Monee, IL
09 October 2022

15512935R00111